GRACE NOTES

[APPOGIATURES]

Grace Notes

[APPOGIATURES]

Jean Cocteau

Translated by

Mary-Sherman Willis

Barbara Goldberg, Series Editor

International Editions
THE WORD WORKS
Washington, D.C.

Cover design: Susan Pearce Design
Translator photograph: Mary Noble Ours

LCCN: 2016957980
ISBN: 978-1-944585-12-9

ACKNOWLEDGMENTS

Some of these translations
have appeared in journals:

Eleven Eleven:
"Hopscotch," "The French Language,"
and "Vienna."

Waxwing:
"Alone," "The Traveler,"
"The Cock Always Crows Three Times,"
and "Crime of Passion."

With special thanks to DeeDee Slewka,
Catherine Guarne, Tommy Bruce,
and Barbara Goldberg.

CONTENTS

PREFACE

Jean Cocteau, the *enfant terrible* of French literature, despite his manifold emotional and physical infirmities, was an artist of prodigious output and prodigious imagination. *Grace Notes* was published in the early 1950s, yet how fresh, even stylish, these prose poems are today, sparkling like little jewels.

These poems are nearly impossible to follow, to understand in a rational way. Don't even try — they are not meant to be understood. Rather, they are as ephemeral as a fleeting glance, or a hint of flavor on the tongue. They move by the music of the language (French), and by Cocteau's flights of fancy as well as by his obsessions. Undoubtedly they are clever. But they are also funny and tragic. Not to mention how enchanting they are no matter the emotional tenor.

And, as is immediately obvious, they are short. That means despite how "light" they are, in terms of only being "grace" notes, they are also dense and compact. You simply have to marvel at their originality and playfulness. What was striking about Cocteau, the man and the artist, was how he retained the playfulness of a child, as well as a child's willful cruelty.

I should mention that when Mary-Sherman Willis first shared these with me, it was love at first sight, or as the French say, "*un coup de foudre*," literally, a bolt of lightning. I didn't have to read more than two or three to know that I wanted to snap them up and present these timeless "grace notes" to a contemporary audience.

You are about to enter Cocteau's capricious world. Prepare to be dazzled.

Barbara Goldberg
Washington, D.C.

*I*NTRODUCTION

Jean Cocteau (1889-1963) was one of the most influential creative figures in the twentieth century Parisian avant-garde. In a career that began with his first published poem at age eighteen in 1908, to the last days of his life, there was no medium he didn't have his hand in, and no important European cultural figure of the time that he didn't know or collaborate with. His circle of friends and collaborators made up a who's who of European artistic life, including Pablo Picasso, Guillaume Apollinaire, Erik Satie, Igor Stravinsky, Sergei Diaghilev, André Gide, Jean Genet, Coco Chanel, Edith Piaf, and Colette.

Notwithstanding his mastery of a huge range of literary, theatrical, and visual media, he considered his works to be a series of variations on the notion of poetry: the poem-film, poem-play, poem-drawing, poem-novel, and so on. As his translator, the poet and essayist Richard Howard, wrote, for Cocteau, "Drawings, films, poems (and the management of their appearance in the world) are an endless stream of objects and texts, of *works and plays* secreted by the poet as the cocoon within which he will stave off death (even if at times it is no more than silence that he defeats)."

Appogiatures represents his late-career work. It mines the imagery and turns of mind he'd developed over the decades. Fans of his films, novels, poetry, illustrations, paintings, sculptures, operas, ballets, and plays will have encountered the temperamental bejeweled countesses, the gods and goddesses, the ghosts moving through walls and mirrors, the talking statues, the fairytale magic, the sometimes cruel wonder. This book distills them into short fantastical scenarios, wildly inventive and emotionally profound.

By the early 1950s when this book was published, Cocteau's reputation was secure (if controversial!) and he was taking steps to stabilize his tumultuous life. He and his recently adopted "son" and lover, Edouard Dermit, had moved into the villa "Santo Sospir" belonging to his patroness, Francine Weisweiller, in St. Jean-Cap-Ferrat, an aristocratic watering hole on the French Riviera near the Italian border. His surrealist film *Orphée* premièred at Cannes in 1950 to acclaim, and won first prize at the Venice International Film Festival. His three-act play, *Bacchus*, would première the next year and be attacked by François Mauriac for blasphemy. In 1952 he wrote most of the poems for his fifteenth book of poems, *Le Chiffre sept*, while cruising on Weisweiller's yacht, *Orphée II*; later that year he had an exhibition of paintings and tapestries. He was firing on all cylinders.

Cocteau was in his early sixties. He had survived two world wars and the Nazi occupation of Paris as an openly gay man; the traumatizing death of his young lover Raymond Radiguet; the end of his long-term relationship with his muse, the actor Jean Marais; and a tenacious opium habit that necessitated frequent sanatorium cures. His health was precarious. In 1946 he had to interrupt the shooting of *La Belle et la bête* (*Beauty and the Beast*) to be hospitalized at the Pasteur Institute. He was so plagued by disfiguring skin ailments — eczema, impetigo, itching, boils, blisters, and swelling — that for some weeks he wore a black veil cut with eyeholes and pinned to his hat. Although free from opium by 1950, death shadowed his life and his work. "You've never seen death?" he wrote. "Look in the mirror every day and you will see it like bees working in a glass hive."

In the summer of 1952, he was editing his 1923 collection of poems *Opéra* for re-issue. Henri Parisot, editor of the *Âge d'or* series of contemporary poetry, had admired that book, in particular the prose poems in the section "The Secret Museum." He proposed a new collection. On a rainy day at the end of July, Cocteau wrote in his diary, "I'm beginning the poems for Parisot's book." This would be his sixteenth book of poems, *Appogiatures*.

Appogiatures was published by Éditions du Rocher in an edition of 1,000 in November of 1953, illustrated with a pencil portrait of the author by Alberto Giacometti and an etching by the German artist Hans Bellmer. Individual poems began to appear in March 1953 in journals. Soon Cocteau was lamenting the "wretched imitations of *Appogiatures* by some poet in the latest issue of *La Parisienne*. . . . My one effort must be to prepare my *Oeuvres complètes*." He was already at work on the poems for his next book, *Clair-obscur*.

An *appoggiatura* (or a grace note) is musical ornament, a little added note before a principal note of melody, to highlight it by delaying it. The prose poems in *Appogiatures* —surreal, cinematic *mise en scenes* — depict a heightened or off-kilter reality caused by some invisible mechanism that might break down at any time, leading to obsession with error.

So it is in the seesawing point of view of a traveler approaching home, in a nightmare chase by the Beauty in which she could "grab his hand, force him to stop and stride regally as in a minuet more terrifying than a ceremonial tribal dance." It could be in the life or death consequences of a bungled game of hopscotch in which a man must face "the white ghost of his ruination." Realities fold into each other. The membranes separating states of consciousness are stretched and punctured. A skater "spun into himself, a speeding tornado, until he became translucent as a spinning propeller, with one difference: he passed into the zone of the visible and / disappeared." The laws of physics and language are pushed to the breaking point, and disaster is always just around the corner.

For Cocteau, death is swift and capricious, only one false move away. But these poems are often absurdly funny and loaded with punning wordplay. There is the ghost who haunts involuntarily, or the café customers who fling their saucers and shred the café awning to read "*FÉ DE LA RADE*," or "stranded fairy." Thanks to the French slang word for a dentist's drill (*fraise*), a dentist grinds his patient's teeth with strawberries. Dread of the dentist's drill becomes delight through a bit of wordplay. Art's effect, a heightened awareness of human existence, is *duende*, Federico García Lorca's term for the spell cast by certain works of art — a gypsy flamenco song, for instance, and its cries of passion and despair. Cocteau in fact salutes Lorca in this book, in "A Farewell Letter to My Friend Federico." But Cocteau's is a Gallic *duende*: witty, cynical, in control of its own logic. Humor and wit underscore tragic reality, taunting it. But the satisfaction mockery gives is short-lived. It is we who are mocked by death, he shows us, whether we try to out-deal the Devil and get the advice, "*You're winning at cards, so you'll have bad luck elsewhere,*" or simply resort to laughing in the dark. In "The Laugh," he shows that laughter can blow up in our faces: "The laugh exploded and injured curious spectators circling it in the street."

These poems serve as warnings: death lies in wait to entrap us, only vaguely aware of it, like the sea that "licked her lips in anticipation." It observes and pursues us like a bossy governess ("How clingy!"). And so we must look for the least sign of it, in its smallest grace notes. Perhaps it is a bugle call announcing an explosion that prevents an accident, or a hero's warnings ignored by a village that would suffer a holocaust. Perhaps it's a gypsy's mournful violin that turns "his grief to soft matter, oily, thick, the consequence of invasions and ruin" and swamps the café customers. Or it's simply the darkness inside the theater of the self.

These are realities of existence in the inevitable course of human life. Like signs along the way, the poems tell us to be aware of death, even as we attend to a creator engaged with it — the poet himself, who will "follow the vanishing day and sing his death song elsewhere."

*A*BOUT THE *T*RANSLATION

The gallows humor of the poems in *Appogiatures* appealed to me when I discovered the book in a small bookstore one summer on the coast of Brittany. I'd been thinking about Jean Cocteau's movie *La Belle et la bête* after spending a week in a friend's garden-shed-guesthouse. The interior of the greenhouse was covered over with grapevines through which you had to walk to get to the bathroom. It was, in my imagination, Belle's boudoir — alive and magic. So I was primed for Cocteau when I came upon the book. I fell in love with the poems' graceful language and relentless wordplay.

Cocteau employs a formal, almost deadpan French that counterpoints his hallucinatory, often ridiculous plots and images. The syntax of his lush sentences, with long sequences of clauses, makes for a filmic storyboard effect. I worked to preserve the pacing and form of those sentences. I also looked into the history of the book's four editions, all with the same publisher, and discovered variations in several poems. For this translation I sought out a 1953 first-edition copy, the only printing in Cocteau's lifetime. In the poem "Alone," I discovered the lovely line, "With a moon that was without being," that was missing in my fourth edition. That first edition had some typographic quirks — inconsistently italicized and punctuated dialogue, for instance — that required case-by-case judgment calls. Cocteau acknowledged his illegible handwriting in letters to friends. No doubt the typesetters and editors at Éditions du Rocher found his hastily assembled manuscript a challenge to decipher.

Trickier were the wordplay and double entendres of his idiomatic expressions, which simply don't convey into English. In English they are plainly surreal; in French they make their own logic. And music. Cocteau makes much use of word repetition and anaphora in his poems — the word "alone" ("*seul*") in "Alone," or the word "strawberry," a pun for a drill bit, in "The Dentist." *A word is a word is a word*, Cocteau seems to be saying, *until a pun steps in*. A hilarious (and naughty) example is the poem "The French Language," in which a countess speaking to her lover in formal literary French unknowingly refers to giving him a blowjob in spoken French; Cocteau skewers the affectations of both aristocratic and academic speech.

In many poems, Cocteau simply lets loose long strings of rhyme words and homophones like improvised jazz. (In the 1920s, in fact, he managed the La Gaya nightclub in Paris, where he played trombone, big drum, castanets, reed-pipe, and car horn in the orchestra.) In a poem like "A Crime of Passion" it pays to read aloud the French: "*S'il était venu et si elle au lieu de venir était allée dans l'allée et n'y était pas allée nue jusqu'à l'île il n'aurait pas été dans la boue jusqu'au bout de l'été pas à pas et debout sur cette île peu sûre seul parmi les saules ennemis.*" The sentence makes no more logical sense in English than it does in the French: "If he had come and she instead of coming had gone into the alley and not gone nude as far as the island he wouldn't have been in the mud step by step till the end of summer and stand on this uncertain island alone amid the enemy willows." The sense is in the sound.

There is a single outlier in this book of prose poems: a poem broken into four rhyming quatrains titled "Prose in Verse." These are alexandrines, twelve-syllable lines with a-b-a-b end-rhyme and random-seeming imagery from a childhood song, from his subconscious, perhaps even from the sounds and sights outside his window. I gave up the syllabic lines and end-rhymes in favor of internal music in English, in keeping with the language and syntax of the original. Otherwise, read these poems as flash fictions, micro-stories, sudden fictions, or as postcards from an invisible known world that you might visit suddenly, and at any time.

Mary-Sherman Willis
Rappahannock County, Virginia

GRACE NOTES

[APPOGIATURES]

SEBALLETUL

Seul debout. Seul assis. Seul couché. Seul sur le gril. Seul écartelé par des chevaux de labour dont il ne voyait que les croupes. Seul pendu et son sperme devint mandragore. Seul dans la vitesse qui n'est pas, dans la minute qui n'est pas, dans l'espace qui n'est pas, dans le temps qui n'est pas, dans l'éternité qui n'est pas, dans le rien qui ne l'est pas, dans le vide plein de boue. Seul dans un bloc de quartz ignoble, dans un iceberg en voyage. Seul avec la solitude qui n'en est pas une. Avec la lune qui fut sans être. Avec ses pas qui n'en sont pas. Avec ce tison qui se croûte et qui brûle au milieu et se croûte et brûle dans un songe qui n'est même pas un songe. Seul avec le sommeil du condamné à mort.

ALONE

Alone standing. Alone sitting. Alone lying down. Alone on the grille. Alone drawn and quartered by workhorses, seeing only their rumps. Alone hanging, ejaculating a mandrake. Alone in the quickness that isn't, the minute that isn't, the space that isn't, in time that isn't, in eternity that isn't, in the nothing that isn't so, in the emptiness full of mud. Alone in a corrupted chunk of quartz, in an iceberg drifting afar. Alone with solitude that isn't one. With a moon that was without being. With his footsteps that aren't footsteps. With this ember that crusts over and burns at its core and crusts and burns in a dream that isn't even a dream. Alone in the sleep of those condemned to death.

LE VOYAGEUR

Plus vite il marchait, plus il approchait de sa maison, plus elle rapetissait, devenait inhabitable. La distance se solidifiait derrière sa marche et le poussait avec le rythme d'une troupe militaire que rien ne presse. Il lui fallait entrer dans cette maison minuscule, ce qui était impossible et devint possible lorsque la muraille militaire s'arrêta. Le voyageur, alors, rapetissa très vite cependant que sa maison grandissait à vue d'œil et qu'une belle jeune fille apparaissait à une fenêtre et riait de son aventure.

THE TRAVELER

The faster he walked, the closer he came to his house, the more it shrank away from him, became uninhabitable. The distance behind his footsteps solidified itself and pressed him forward with the cadence of marching troops that nothing could hurry. He had to enter that minuscule house, which was impossible, yet became possible once the phalanx of soldiers came to a halt. The traveler then shrank rapidly even as his house swelled visibly and in a window a beautiful young girl appeared, laughing at his predicament.

LE COQ CHANTE TOUJOURS TROIS FOIS

Il courait à perdre haleine, suivi par la beauté. Il se retourna. Elle approchait, laide à faire peur. Elle grimaçait au soleil et par l'effort de sa course. Il craignait qu'elle ne le rattrapât et ne lui prît la main, l'obligeant à une halte, à une marche noble pareille aux menuets plus inquiétants que les danses d'un cérémonial sauvage. Il avait toujours redouté ces danses pompeuses sous la montagne de guano des perruques Louis XIV. La beauté s'essoufflait à le suivre, à crier: «*Vous déplacez mes lignes*» Et comme personne ne la reconnaissait, la foule hurlait: *Au voleur!* En fin de course il y eut un mur. Il devint facile de traquer et de lapider le malheureux jusqu'à ce que la beauté, l'ayant rejoint, dise: «Je m'étais trompée. Je m'en excuse. Je ne connais pas cet homme.»

THE COCK ALWAYS CROWS THREE TIMES

He gasped for air as he ran, pursued by Beauty. He turned back. She was catching up, fearsomely ugly. She grimaced in the sun and with the effort of the chase. He was afraid she would catch up with him, grab his hand, force him to stop and stride regally as in a minuet more terrifying than a ceremonial tribal dance. He always dreaded the pompous dances under those Louis XIV wigs like mountains of birdshit. Beauty faltered as she followed, screaming, "You're throwing me off step!" And because no one recognized her, the crowd howled, *Stop, thief!* At the end of the race there was a wall. It was easy to trap and stone the unfortunate man, but just then Beauty caught up with him and said, "I made a mistake. I'm sorry. I don't know this man."

LA MARELLE

A cloche-pied, après avoir, à genoux, tracé les lignes de craie d'une marelle qui se ramifiait dans les rues, il commença le parcours interminable où la moindre faute devait ruiner son pouvoir. A cloche-pied, il pensait, calculait et son cœur battait la chamade. Car il savait bien que cette craie sur les pavés simulait un plan d'une puissance géométrique équivalente à celle des lieux invisibles dont il reproduisait la topographie. Et il suffisait d'un faux pas de l'homme qui sautille, une distraction (qui lui ferait, par exemple, poser par terre le pied gauche) pour que les prérogatives du lieu simulé devinssent nulles et s'évaporassent. Pour que les antennes de l'homme à cloche-pied perdissent leur vertu, ne fussent que de simples poils sur les jambes. C'est l'angoisse de perdre l'équilibre qui communiquait à son visage cet air de crucifié épouvantant les femmes sur le seuil des portes. Les enfants pleuraient. Les mères les emmenaient, s'enfermaient chez elles, se signaient dans les vestibules.

Un chien noir déboucha d'une impasse. Il bouscula l'homme. Une seconde le pied gauche toucha la septième case. Alors le coq chanta. L'homme baissa la tête et, la figure dans les mains, s'assit sur une marche en face du spectre blanc de sa ruine.

HOPSCOTCH

Hopping, after being on his knees in the street to trace the branching chalk-lines of a game of hopscotch, he began his interminable course where the smallest mistake would sap away his power. Hopping, he thought, he calculated, his heart pounding wildly. Because he knew very well that this chalk on this pavement represented the geometrical power of invisible places whose topography he was replicating here. It would take only one misstep of the hopping man, one distraction (causing him, for instance, to place his left foot on the ground), for the primacy of the imagined terrain to become null and void. For the hopping man's antennae to lose their effect, to become simply the hairs on his legs. The expression on his face at the anguish of losing his balance was of a man crucified, and it terrified the women in their doorways. Children were crying. Mothers rushed to bring them inside, lock the doors and cross themselves in their vestibules.

A black dog emerged from a dead end. He brushed against the man. Briefly, his left foot touched the seventh square. A cock crowed. The man lowered his face to his hands, sat down on the curb before the white ghost of his ruination.

LE PATINEUR

S'élança le patineur sur la piste vierge où il lui fallait reproduire avec ses pieds armés l'inextricable méandre d'une ligne qu'il portait en lui et dont rien ne délivrait son âme ligotée et interrogée par la police. Il serait libre s'il burinait à toute vitesse une surface où l'entaille projetait des copeaux de neige. Chef-d'œuvre que les ensuite, le précédaient et l'invitaient à les rejoindre. Les bras croisés, il penchait, se redressait, filait, virait, repartait, attentif à ne jamais interrompre sa calligraphie. Pendant une heure il en boucla les pleins et les déliés sans commettre une faute. Soudain, au centre de la piste, et d'abord immobile, ses bras d'épouvantail étendus, il tourna sur lui-même en un cyclone accéléré jusqu'à le rendre translucide et tel qu'une hélice mais avec cette différence qu'il passa la zone du visible et
disparut.

THE SKATER

The skater launched himself onto the virgin ice, compelled to reproduce with his bladed feet the inextricable meander of a line that he carried inside himself, trapping his soul, straightjacketed as it was and under police interrogation. He would be free if he chiseled at great speed a surface from which the gash threw off shavings of snow. A masterpiece that the spectators applauded as if it were a simple acrobatic exercise. Sometimes he left behind several images of his body that would rejoin him, then precede him and invite him to join them. With crossed arms, he leaned, straightened up, sped ahead fast, turned, took off, careful never to break off his calligraphy. For an hour he inscribed his curled upstrokes and downstrokes without one error. Suddenly, in the middle of the rink and standing still, his scarecrow arms outstretched, he spun into himself, a speeding tornado, until he became translucent as a spinning propeller, with one difference: he passed through the zone of the visible and
disappeared.

PLACES RETENUES

À la colère légitime des trois passagers de l'appareil qui allait être réduit en miettes, le destin, en uniforme d'Air-France, opposait l'entêtement d'une administration qui range à gauche ceux qu'elle accepte et à droite ceux qu'elle refuse, avec le style des casernes auquel il serait naïf de répondre par la révolte. Non pas que ces passagers fussent blâmables de trouver injuste que des personnes n'ayant pas retenu de places à l'avance occupassent les leurs, mais perdissent le calme en face d'un uniforme et voulussent s'opposer à ce que ces personnes tinssent à mourir coûte que coûte, par l'entremise il est vrai de recommandations spéciales et en quelque sorte de passe-droits.

A quoi servent les menaces, les plaintes écrites à des bureaux surchargés de travail par l'enquête sur les responsables du sinistre qui devait avoir lieu dans quinze minutes, sinistre dont nous ne pûmes, du reste, que louer ces trois messieurs de vouloir sauver des victimes innocentes, sauf en ce qui concerne l'indélicatesse de prendre frauduleusement des places retenues.

RESERVED SEATS

To the legitimate anger of the three passengers on the airplane that would be reduced to smithereens, fate, in an Air France uniform, came up against the stubbornness of a bureaucracy that directs to the left those it accepts and to the right those it denies, in a barracks-like fashion it would be naïve to oppose. Not that we should blame these passengers for finding it unjust that people who hadn't reserved seats were occupying theirs, would lose their cool when confronted by a uniform and challenge the people holding on to the death, whatever the cost, having taken advantage, it is true, of special approvals and some sort of privileges.

Of what use are threats, written complaints to offices overburdened by the investigation into those responsible for the disaster scheduled to take place in fifteen minutes, disaster for which we should, by the way, commend those three gentlemen for wanting to save those victims, innocents except for the incivility of taking reserved seats fraudulently.

PRAIRIE DE PLUMES

L'Enfer était une prairie de barbes de plumes dont le terrible apparut à ce pauvre homme sous un aspect d'usage encore incompréhensible. Cette attente lui devint insupportable au point qu'il préférait imaginer un supplice qui serait par exemple un éternel chatouillement de la plante des pieds. L'attente se prolongeait. Le pauvre homme comprit alors que son supplice serait cette attente, que les barbes des plumes ne prendraient jamais une autre signification à ses yeux et qu'il serait torturé par le simple frémissement de cette prairie de plumes énigmatiques.

FIELD OF QUILLS

Hell was a field of feather quills where the terrible appeared to this poor man incomprehensibly pointless. His wait there became so unbearable he preferred to imagine some other agony, for example the eternal tickling of the soles of his feet. The wait prolonged. The poor man then understood that this waiting would be his torture, that the quills would never take on a significance to him other than quills, and that his torment would simply be the quivering of this field of enigmatic feathers.

SON DU COR

Un cor de chasse traversait le mur, ralenti par la difficulté qu'il avait à faire son chemin dans la brique et dans les nébuleuses de l'âme. De telle sorte que ce cor et ce corps formaient une pâte dégoûtante. Il restait de la poudre de brique et de la bave des limaces d'une forêt où le cerf se déguise mal en arbre.

Enroulés dans ce cor de chasse, Roland, Tristan, moururent du boa qui les étouffait de sa boue ingénieuse, et ce n'était rien jusqu'à l'aventure d'une gueule pompant ce *sac de son* et, l'ayant pompé, le digérant au bord des marécages du crépuscule.

SOUND OF THE HORN

A hunting horn traversed the wall, bogged down as it made its way through the brick and the soul's nebulas. So much so that horn and body turned into a disgusting paste. Brick powder remained and slug slime from a forest where a stag is ill-disguised as a tree.

Coiled in this hunting horn, Roland and Tristan suffocated to death in the boa constrictor's ingenious mud; this was nothing to the story of a mouth sucking up its *sack of sound*, and having sucked, digests at the edge of the swamps of twilight.

CRIME PASSIONNEL

S'il était venu et si elle au lieu de venir était allée dans l'allée et n'y était pas allée nue jusqu'à l'île il n'aurait pas été dans la boue jusqu'au bout de l'été pas à pas et debout sur cette île peu sûre seul parmi les saules ennemis. Elle aurait eu des ailes. Il aurait tû l'orée du bois et l'or et la biche aux abois. Il et elle seraient riches sans cette boue sur les chaussures et sans le sang et ce 7 et ce 10 et ce verre et ces indices. Ils auraient eu chaud sans plus. Un non-lieu au lieu de ce verdict. Il s'en serait allé par l'allée des statues sans lire et sans salir ses chaussures de chasse et sans ce vert de la mousse sur ses moustaches et sans cette tache de sang qui les tue.

CRIME OF PASSION

If he had come and she instead of coming had gone into the alley and not gone nude as far as the island he wouldn't have been in the mud step by step till the end of summer and stand on this uncertain island alone amid the enemy willows. She'd have wings. She'd have hushed the forest's edge and the gold and the doe at bay. He and she would be rich without that mud on their shoes and without the blood, that seven, that ten, this glass, and these clues. They'd have felt the heat and nothing more. A case dismissed instead of a verdict. He'd have gone down an alley of statues without reading and without dirtying his hunting shoes and without this green moss on his moustache and without this bloodstain killing them.

LA SOIRÉE DE SAUVEGARDES

C'était sinistre qu'il grimaçât, mais de douleur ce fut pire. Des fils de fer rouges jaillissaient de ses yeux et se terminaient par des balles gluantes. La bouche était un égout de tendre haine. La musique de cet *Œdipe-roi* était d'un certain Eddy Proah et ce nom avait décidé de la commande en Amérique.

Les enfants regardaient avec angoisse le spectacle que la comtesse avait eu l'idée saugrenue de monter dans le théâtre du parc de Sauvegardes. Une petite fille était morte de peur. Sa famille l'emportait, accompagnée d'un cortège funèbre. Œdipe criait: « *Funeste! Funeste!* » et son œil s'allongeait en forme d'œil de langouste, en forme de télescope, en forme de cornet à surprises. Erreur curieuse d'une femme de goût (veuve d'un aveugle) qui sanglotait dans la serre entre les pots de géraniums et le passe-boules.

SOIRÉE IN THE PRESERVE

It was ominous that he grimaced, but the pain made it worse. Red wires gushed from his eyes, ending in sticky balls. The mouth was a sewer-hole of tender hatred. The music of this *Oedipus Rex* was by a certain Eddy Proah, the name picked on order from America.

In anguish, the children watched the performance, which the countess had the half-baked idea to stage in the theater in the Nature Preserve. A little girl was frightened to death. Her family carried her, followed by a funeral procession. Oedipus cried, "*Disaster! Disaster!*" and his eye elongated into a lobster eye, a telescope, an ice-cream cone. Curious error for a woman of taste (a blind man's widow) who sobbed in the hothouse between pots of geraniums and a children's game of ball-toss.

LA LANGUE FRANÇAISE

« Vous ne supposiez tout de même pas que je le susse! » dit la marquise avec une réelle noblesse. Mais le jeune drôle connaissait mal la langue française. Il ricana et accusa la marquise de dire des obscénités. *« Moi? »* Ce *moi* fut un chef-d'œuvre. La marquise se dressait dans une robe de percaline jaune brodée d'iris noirs en jais et de jacinthes en turquoises. Sa traîne commençait cette robe et il semblait que ses étoffes montassent du sol pour s'enrouler autour des chevilles, des cuisses, des fesses, du ventre, de la taille, et mourir au bord des seins. La marquise était moins jeune que ne l'avouait son passeport mais belle de colère en face du jeune drôle à qui elle avait eu la faiblesse d'accorder ses faveurs. Son rire la saccageait, saccageait ses iris, ses jacinthes, ses turquoises. On eut dit une grande vague furieuse et jaune. « Misérable! » s'écria la marquise et superbement elle dégrafa cette vague d'étoffes. Toute nue, n'ayant que ses perles au cou, d'un geste théâtral sa main désignait la porte. Le jeune drôle baissa la tête et quitta le château. Alors, victime de l'amour et de la langue française, la marquise s'abattit dans une sombre écume multicolore.

THE FRENCH LANGUAGE

"You don't really suppose I should have known it!" said the marquise with true nobility. But the young fool didn't understand the French language well. He sniggered and accused the marquise of speaking obscenities. "*Me?*" That *me* was a masterpiece. She wore a dress of yellow percale embroidered with jet-black irises and bluebells in turquoises. The dress began at her train, winding up from the floor, around her ankles, her thighs, her rear, her belly, around her waist, and died out at her breasts. The marquise was older than her passport admitted, but beautiful in her rage against the young fool to whom she'd accorded her favors in a moment of weakness. His laugh wrecked her, wrecked the irises, bluebells, and turquoises. A tsunami, yellow and furious. "Wretch!" cried the marquise and magnificently unfastened that wave of fabric. Naked, only her pearls at her throat, she theatrically showed him the door. The young fool lowered his head and left the chateau. And so, a victim of love and the French language, the marquise collapsed into dark mottled seafoam.

TEL MAÎTRE, TEL VALET

«Que faites-vous de beau?» dit le diable en battant les cartes. Voulait-il me distraire et les distribuer à son avantage? «Mais je ne fais rien,» répondis-je. — «Vous avez l'air heureux, calme, tout ce qu'il ne faudrait pas être pour faire quelque chose et quelque chose de beau.» Je lui demandai s'il conseillait que je tirasse le diable par la queue. — «Ne vous en sortez pas par une boutade. Vous gagnez aux cartes. C'est donc que les autres chances vous trompent. Je ne saurais assez vous conseiller de perdre. Bien que perdre exprès . . . Et, en outre,» (il rit très fort) «Vous pensez à autre chose. A quoi ? C'est le comble. Tenez, avec mon valet de pique je prends votre as de cœur.»

LIKE MASTER, LIKE VALET

"What clever thing are you doing?" said the devil, shuffling the cards. Did he want to distract me and deal them to his advantage? "I'm not doing anything," I replied. — "You seem happy, calm, which you shouldn't be if you were up to something, something clever." I asked if he'd advise me to pull the devil by the tail. — "Don't get out of it by joking. You're winning at cards, so you'll have bad luck elsewhere. I strongly advise you to lose. But not on purpose... And besides" (he laughed hard), "now you're thinking of something else. What could it be? Well that beats it. Here, my jack of spades takes your ace of hearts."

LA PIANISTE

L'accident qui aurait pu arriver se déroula en fugue de Bach extrêmement bien exécutée par une pianiste qui savait que la moindre fausse note déterminerait l'accident. Il y avait trente personnes dans la carlingue. L'hôtesse de l'air souriait et distribuait des friandises. La pianiste sentait son cœur battre à se rompre. Il battait jusqu'au bout de ses doigts agiles et vieux. Elle n'osait les regarder exécutant la fugue en ré qu'il ne s'agissait pas d'exécuter avec brio mais avec une scrupuleuse exactitude. La pianiste calculait. Elle pensait à son fils qui était trompette et devait concourir au Festival des Caves en Octobre. Il jouait de la trompette et de malchance car les juges estimaient que son jeu était trop sentimental. C'est qu'il pensait à sa mère pianiste et à cette fugue d'où dépendait, sans qu'elles s'en doutassent, la vie de trente personnes remplissant des fiches ou feuilletant des magazines.

« *La moindre fausse note!* » Il se répétait cette phrase et la pianiste se disait: « *Le mécanisme ! Le mécanisme!* » Car son fils tenait d'elle une sensibilité ridicule. On avait recommandé de ne pas applaudir. Toutes ces circonstances permirent au pilote de se poser sur l'aéroport.

THE PIANIST

The accident that could have happened unfurled like a Bach fugue played expertly by a pianist who knew that the least false note determines the outcome. There were thirty people in the cabin. The stewardess smiled as she passed around sweets. The pianist felt her heart beat to bursting. It beat to the tips of her fingers, nimble and old. She didn't dare look at them playing the fugue in D, not to be executed con brio, but with scrupulous precision. She calculated. She thought of her son, a trumpeter who would compete at the Festival of the Caves in October. The judges unfortunately thought his playing too sentimental. He was thinking of his pianist mother and this fugue upon which depended — they had no inkling of it — the lives of thirty people filling out forms or leafing though magazines.

"The least false note!" he repeated, while the pianist said to herself, *"The mechanism! The mechanism!"* Her son had inherited her ridiculous susceptibility. They requested the audience hold their applause. Taken together these conditions allowed the pilot to land the plane on the runway.

LE DENTISTE

« J'ai pour vous de nouvelles fraises, » dit le dentiste. Le client pensa que ces fraises étaient pour l'endormir car chacun sait que les fraises contiennent de l'éther et endorment ceux qui en abusent.

Les fraises du dentiste tournaient à toute vitesse et son pied en actionnait le mécanisme. « Mes fraises, » dit-il, « sont des fraises à pied, car notre ville n'a pas encore le courant électrique. » Ces fraises à pied étaient délicieuses. Le client ouvrait grande la bouche et le dentiste ne ménageait pas les fraises qui étaient petites mais d'un goût plus vif que les grosses fraises qu'on force et qui sont pleines d'eau.

Elles coûtaient fort cher. Le client s'exécuta. Il estimait que le jeu en valait la chandelle. « Vos fraises, » déclara-t-il, en payant le dentiste, « étaient excellentes. Loin d'attaquer les dents par leur sucre, elles les soignent. Je compte en cultiver un plant dans mon jardin. » Depuis, les fraises à pied du client lui valent des revenus considérables, et il garde une grande reconnaissance au dentiste auquel il ne manquera pas d'en envoyer une corbeille à chaque récolte.

THE DENTIST

"I have fresh strawberries for you," says the dentist. The patient thought they were to make him sleep, because everyone knows that strawberries contain ether and will put those who abuse them to sleep.

The dentist's strawberries whirred and his foot controlled the action. "My strawberries," he says, "are foot-operated since our town doesn't have electricity yet." These foot-operated strawberries were delicious. The patient opened his mouth wide and the dentist did not spare the strawberries, which were small but more flavorful than the big watery ones grown under cover.

They were very expensive. The patient settled up, figuring the cost was well worth it. "Your strawberries," said he, "were excellent. Rather that ruining my teeth with sugar, they healed them. I plan to grow a patch in my garden." Ever since, those foot-operated strawberries have been bringing him a tidy income, and he shows his gratitude by sending the dentist a basket-full at each harvest.

LE COCHER DE ROME

Partant de ce phantasme des personnes qui prétendent avoir déjà vécu d'autres vies et ne se souviennent que d'illustres, nous soupçonnâmes le cocher du fiacre qui nous promenait dans Rome, à certains indices et à une pente qui dirigeait toujours son cheval vers la Maison Dorée, nous le soupçonnâmes, dis-je, dressés par l'école du songe où l'extraordinaire cesse de l'être et, je le répète, à certains indices et à un mélange de gênes réciproques, celle qui accompagne une découverte pénible et celle d'être découvert, bref, pendant que les sabots du cheval et les roues faisaient leur bruit de corbillard dans des ruelles pleines de soutanes écarlates et que Rome prenait cette couleur orangée par quoi elle se distingue de toute autre capitale, nous soupçonnâmes, nous eûmes la certitude — certitude si forte que nous faillîmes descendre du fiacre — que ce cocher était Néron, extrêmement ennuyé de se reconnaître, à force d'avoir été *reconnu*.

THE ROMAN COACHMAN

Starting with the fantasy of people claiming past lives but recollecting only the famous, we suspected the coachman of the carriage taking us around Rome, given certain clues and that his route always seemed to direct his horse toward the Domus Aurea, we suspected him, as I say, trained as we are in the school of dreams where nothing is extraordinary, and, I repeat, because of certain clues and a combination of discomfitures: that of a painful discovery and that of being discovered, in brief, while the horse's hooves and the wheels made their hearse-sounds down narrow streets full of scarlet cassocks, and because Rome took on that orangey color that distinguishes it from all other capitals, we suspected, we were certain — so certain we almost got out of the carriage — that this coachman was Nero himself, highly annoyed to recognize himself, having been *recognized*.

VIENNE

Il était de toute évidence que le vieux tzigane du Café de Vienne où nous échouâmes avec le ministre se vidait de sa substance et que cette substance, devenue visible, se déroulait, s'enroulait, se tordait, se nouait, se dénouait, avec la lourde agilité du miel qui coule sur du miel. Substance molle, grasse, épaisse, en quoi se changeaient ses plaintes, justifiées par des invasions et par la ruine. Notre table menaçait d'être un îlot entouré de cette pâte. Quelques dames, hérissées du rayonnement de châtaigne de leurs pierreries, les coudes sur la nappe, l'ovale du visage entre leurs mains et l'œil vague, ne sentaient pas encore les gluantes écharpes qui surchargeaient leurs épaules nues. Le ministre, le regard aux anges, battait la mesure, empâté jusqu'aux cuisses. D'autres consommateurs, plus lucides, et n'osant se plaindre, montaient sur les banquettes. Le vieux tzigane continuait. Les épaules nues le mettaient en verve. Il sanglotait. Il se vidait sous le regard effrayé de l'accordéoniste et de la caissière. La caissière, habitant comme un refuge, risquait d'être atteinte après les autres victimes de cette pâte qui faisait ressembler la salle à une fosse pleine de serpents. Seul le tzigane paraissait échapper à sa propre perte et en tirer une plainte déchirante. Mais il s'arrêta de jouer, après la glissade mortelle de l'archet sur une corde et, avec une vélocité incroyable, toute cette pâte réintégra son corps, vida la salle, laissa les convives stupides, dans des postures de mannequins.

VIENNA

It was obvious the old gypsy at the Café Vienna, where we fetched up with the minister, was emptying himself of substance, and that substance, now visible, was winding, unwinding, twisting, knotting, unknotting itself, with the heavy suppleness of honey pouring into honey. His grief converted to soft matter, oily, thick, the consequence of invasions and ruin. Our table was an islet engulfed by this stuff. Several women, bristling like chestnut burrs with gemstones, elbows on the tablecloth, the ovals of their faces held between their hands and their eyes vague, didn't yet feel the sticky shawls burdening their bare shoulders. The minister beat time, eyes to heaven and sunk in the goop to his thighs. Other customers, more attentive but not daring to complain, climbed on their seats. The old gypsy played on. Bare shoulders put him in brilliant form. He sobbed. He emptied himself under the frightened gaze of the accordionist and the cashier. She in her safe haven would be the last of the victims swamped by the glop turning the room into a snake pit. The gypsy alone escaped his own ruin, extracting a heart-rending cry from it. But with a fatal stroke of the bow he stopped playing. Then with astonishing speed the ooze returned to his body and emptied the room, leaving the guests stupid, posed like mannequins.

COMPTE RENDU SPORTIF DE POÉSIE

Un mot vient de prendre la tête. Un verbe le suit de près et oblige à la pose du point final. Mais non! Mais non! Une simple lettre accourt vaincre la majuscule. Le point se sauve. Dans une échappée magnifique une virgule remonte. Le vide ne bouge pas au centre. Aussitôt le mot de tête l'a vu. Il ne se trouvait pas où il devait être. Il pousse les syllabes à une manœuvre tournante qui se change en offensive, offensive à laquelle personne ne pouvait s'attendre et qui oblige le rejet à perdre l'équilibre. Il tombe, entraînant toute la strophe dans sa chute. Véritable bagarre d'où le mot supprimé s'élance et détermine les autres à se relever et à se précipiter avant que le mot de tête ne s'en aperçoive. Le mot supprimé passe à gauche et l'arbitre annonce un coup franc au bénéfice d'une rime qui semblait faiblir. Elle retrouve sa forme. Malheureusement elle passe trop haut et la reprise entraîne les adjectifs qui attendaient une occasion de jouer un rôle dans la partie.

POETRY SPORTS REPORT

A word just took the lead. A verb follows close behind and forces the placement of the period. But no! But no! One simple letter rushes to beat the capital. The period gets away. In a magnificent breakaway, a comma catches up. The opening in the center doesn't budge. The lead word sees it right away, not where it was supposed to be. It propels the syllables in a turning maneuver that becomes an offensive no one could have expected, and which tips the enjambment off balance. It drops, dragging the whole stanza with it. It's a real fight when the deleted word dashes off and induces the others to scramble before the lead word notices. The deleted word passes to the left and the referee announces a free kick for the rhyme, which seems to weaken. It recoups. Unfortunately it passes too high. Resumption of play drags off the adjectives, which have been waiting for a chance to play a role in the match.

L'INSTITUTRICE

Cette vieille institutrice était sans excuses. Par exemple, elle empêchait les petites filles d'aller le Dimanche au cirque sous prétexte que, toute la semaine, elles n'avaient travaillé que dans cette attente. Ou bien elle disait: «Regarde où tu marches» et les poussait dans les oubliettes de cette école construite sur les souterrains du duc de Guise. Ou encore elle se déguisait en spectre du duc et traversait les dortoirs.

Il y eut des mutineries. Des rougeoles et des scarlatines de révolte, qui couvaient sous le couvercle de la marmite.

Un matin, on trouva l'institutrice clouée sur la porte de chêne avec une pancarte qui affichait ces mots en lettres gothiques: MERCY BEAUCOUP.

THE TEACHER

That old teacher had no excuses. She had, for example, forbidden the little girls from going to the circus on Sunday, under the pretext that they'd worked all week only in expectation of it. Or she would say, "Look where you're walking," and shove them into the school dungeons built into the Duc de Guise's underground passages. Or she would disguise herself as the duke's ghost and roam the dormitories.

There were mutinies. Measles and scarlet fever rebellions stewed under the lid of the cooking pot.

One morning they found the teacher nailed to the old oak door and a placard on which were scrawled these words in Gothic letters: MERCY BEAUCOUP.

FÊTES GALANTES

Idéale. Elle est idéale. C'était la rumeur des vagues du cotillon où les jeunes filles devaient se mettre nues, échanger leurs robes. Les mères souriaient par-dessus des éventails où étaient peintes différentes scènes du massacre des Innocents et des courses de taureaux avec peignes, capes rouges, cous noirs fleuris de roses trémières. Les bougies des lustres fondaient et penchaient, suscitant des fous rires étouffés dans la troupe des jeunes filles nues. Des domestiques portaient en équilibre des plateaux de métal sur lesquels les glaces chaudes coulaient et maculaient leurs uniformes d'azur et d'or. C'était splendide. Digne des époques lointaines où les rois ne dédaignaient pas de danser la gavotte avec bergères tissées au petit point et jeunes joueurs de clarinette fort débraillés sur la mousse. On ne saurait assez encourager ces fêtes galantes naïves et virginales, assez dire et redire ce qu'elles apportent de neuf dans un monde amoureux des naufrages.

FÊTES GALANTES

Ideal. She is ideal – the word swirled though the fancy dress ball where the young girls had to strip naked and swap dresses. Mothers smiled over their fans painted with various scenes from the Massacre of the Innocents, scenes of bullfights, with combs, red capes, black necks blooming with hollyhocks. Candles in the chandeliers melted and drooped, eliciting stifled giggles from the troupe of naked girls. Servants balanced metal trays where warm ices dripped, staining their blue and gold uniforms. It was splendid. Worthy of long-ago époques and kings not averse to dancing a gavotte with needlepointed shepherdesses and utterly disheveled young clarinet players on the moss. One can't encourage these naïve and virginal courting parties enough, or emphasize enough the novelty they bring to a world in love with shipwrecks.

VILLE D'EAUX

Le centre de gravité. Voilà ce qui manquait à cette petite ville estivale avec ses forteresses où veillent des sentinelles en robes de nymphe. Le centre de gravité, la rose des vents, les points cardinaux. Elle s'y embrouillait, mouillait son crayon, rêveuse, avec sa langue. Trop jeune ou trop vieille pour faire des devoirs de vacances. Elle y perdait l'équilibre, semblable aux archiduchesses qui s'abattent sur des poufs après une valse de Strauss, pareille à elle-même, trop ressemblante en quelque sorte, sans le signe d'intelligence un peu fou du génie. Elle croyait que ses plate-bandes, ses remparts, ses digues, son kiosque à musique suffiraient à la maintenir droite, remplaceraient avantageusement le socle du centre de gravité qui lui manque. Et son casino vide pompait ses dernières forces, lui mettait autour des yeux ce cerne mauve, privilège du crépuscule et des anémones.

THE SPA

The center of gravity. That's what was missing in this little summer town, with its fortress, its sentinels dressed like nymphs. Center of gravity, compass rose, four cardinal points. Muddled, she wet the tip of her pencil dreamily with her tongue. Too young, too old for vacation homework. She'd lost her balance, much like archduchesses collapsing on poufs after a Strauss waltz, true to form, in a way, too much alike, no sign of the slightly mad intelligence of genius. She believed that her flowerbeds, ramparts, seawall, her bandstand were enough to hold her up, would stand in for the center of gravity she lacked. Her empty casino had sucked away the last of her strength, put purple circles around her eyes, the color of twilight, of anemones.

UNE TRÈS CURIEUSE EXPOSITION

On annonce à B. une très curieuse exposition de photographies prises par des enfants. Les familles ont eu l'idée charmante de confier des appareils de photographie à des enfants malhabiles à s'en servir. Il en résulte de véritables petits chefs-d'œuvre.

Le seul reproche qu'on puisse faire, disent les critiques, serait une tendance fâcheuse vers un retour à l'impressionnisme. Le jour de l'ouverture, le Ministre de l'Éducation Nationale a décoré de la Légion d'Honneur, le jeune Jean-Claude F., âgé d'un an, pour sa remarquable « *nature morte* ».

A VERY CURIOUS EXHIBITION

Announcing a very curious exhibition at B. of children's photographs. Their families had the charming idea of giving cameras to children with no skill at using them. The results were true little masterpieces.

The only criticism we might make, say the critics, would be of an irritating tendency to return to Impressionism. On opening day, the National Education Minister awarded the Legion of Honor to young Jean-Claude F., aged one year, for his remarkable *"still life."*

LE FANTÔME RÉALISTE

L'ennui de ce fantôme était d'être réaliste et même jugé néo-réaliste par d'autres fantômes abstraits. Par exemple, il arrivait souvent que des personnes normales et vivantes le prissent pour une personne normale et vivante et lui adressassent la parole. Alors il disparaissait d'un seul coup, sans avoir recours à ce fondu-enchaîné cher aux cinéastes.

Les personnes normales et vivantes croyaient qu'une personne normale et vivante, en chair et en os, était entrée chez elles et avait quitté leur chambre.

Malgré toutes ses tentatives, le fantôme réaliste ne parvenait pas à la transparence, au vague, au flou, au style. Son rêve eût été de se rendre méconnaissable. Sa tristesse devint telle qu'il résistait même à la tentation d'apparaître. Mais, parfois, il apparaissait sans le vouloir. Son costume d'époque le faisait prendre pour un acteur dont on s'étonnait seulement qu'il errât comme dans une coulisse à travers les salles nocturnes d'un château d'Écosse.

THE REALIST GHOST

The ghost's trouble was that it was realistic, considered even neo-realist by other abstract ghosts. For instance, normal living people often mistook it for a normal living person, and spoke to it. Then it would disappear all at once, without resorting to the slow-dissolve so dear to filmmakers.

Normal living people believed a normal living person, of flesh and bones, had entered and left their room.

Despite all its attempts, the realist ghost couldn't achieve transparency, in vagueness, fuzziness, or style. Its dream was to make itself unrecognizable. It became so unhappy it even resisted the temptation to appear. But sometimes it appeared despite itself. In period costume, it was mistaken for an actor wandering in by surprise, as if gliding behind the scenes through the nighttime rooms of a Scottish castle.

OSCAR

« *J'ai l'Oscar* ». Ainsi s'exprimait le film réaliste. Il s'estimait surréaliste et même opportuniste par rapport à quelque tribunal invisible devant lequel il devait comparaître sous peu mais il ne savait où. On craignait ce tribunal encore qu'aucune des personnes informées qui en parlaient ne le connussent ni ne l'imaginassent. L'Oscar ne pèserait pas lourd en face de ces juges dont le film réaliste ou surréaliste ou opportuniste cherchait à deviner la jurisprudence. Il s'y perdait, enroulé dans les boîtes où il digérait l'Oscar, pareil à ce sombre reptile d'un film (lui, documentaire) engloutissant un reptile pâle dont on ne voyait en fin de compte que la tête plate criant silencieusement au secours. Il ne savait s'il lui serait favorable ou défavorable d'attendre. Il se demandait ce que durerait cette attente. Si les juges ne l'avaient pas jugé dans un monde où ses boîtes n'offraient pas plus d'importance qu'une boîte de conserves. Il se répétait avec amertume: « *L'Oscar. L'Oscar. J'ai L'Oscar* ». Et il songeait à cet Oscar célèbre, à ce cadavre d'Oscar qu'une muse préraphaélite veillait toute seule dans sa pauvre chambre d'hôtel de la rive gauche.

OSCAR

"I got the Oscar." So declared the realist film. Shortly to appear before a kind of invisible panel of judges, not certain where, it considered itself surrealist or even opportunist. Even more nerve-wracking, this tribunal was made up of experts who would speak about it knowing nothing about it, or even able to imagine it. The Oscar couldn't carry much weight before these judges whose verdict the realist or surrealist or opportunist film can't guess. Lost in wondering, coiled up in its cans, it digested the Oscar like some dark reptile of a film (itself, a documentary) devouring another pale reptile, with only the flat head revealed, silently crying for help. It couldn't decide if waiting was good or bad. It wondered how long the wait would last. Or whether the judges were judging it in a world in which its film cans were less important than a can of preserves. It said to itself bitterly over and over, *"The Oscar. The Oscar. I got the Oscar."* It dreamed of this famous Oscar, of this corpse of Oscar watched over by a pre-Raphaelite muse alone in her poor hotel room on the Left Bank.

LA MER

Septembre bousculait Août, mais où? C'était la question que se posaient les baigneurs réfugiés dans les cabines. Ces cabines étaient des cercueils à roulettes avec des ouvertures en forme d'as de carreau et peintes comme les guérites où les sentinelles gardent la mort. La mer se pourléchait à l'avance. Elle attendait Novembre, son camarade, complice de ses mauvais coups.

THE SEA

September pushed aside August, but where? That was the question the bathers asked themselves, taking refuge in their cabins. These cabins were wheeled coffins with openings shaped like the ace of diamonds and painted like sentry boxes where sentries guard death. The sea licked her lips in anticipation. She waited for November, her comrade and partner in dirty tricks.

SOUCOUPES VOLANTES

Les soucoupes volaient à la terrasse du Café de la Rade. Les garçons n'y pouvaient rien et disaient que ce n'étaient pas des soucoupes mais des mirages. Terrible vol silencieux de soucoupes que les consommateurs se lançaient à la tête, qui ne touchaient personne et disparaissaient silencieusement vers l'est.

Des femmes pleuraient. Des hommes, révoltés, criaient au scandale et voulurent se faire rembourser les consommations qui tachaient les costumes de toile blanche. D'autres craignaient que les soucoupes ne revinssent et ne les frappassent. On ne s'y reconnaissait plus. Le store pendait. *FÉ DE LA RADE* était tout ce qu'on pouvait lire sur la banderole en fuite sur la digue. Les photographes prétendaient avoir des preuves. Mais lorsqu'ils développèrent les preuves-épreuves, aucune soucoupe n'avait été prise par leurs appareils.

FLYING SAUCERS

Saucers flew at the terrace of the Café de la Rade. Waiters couldn't do anything about it, and told everyone they weren't saucers, but mirages. A terrible silent flight of saucers that the customers flung at each other's heads, but struck no one and disappeared just as silently to the east.

Women wept. The men, horrified, cried scandal and demanded refunds for the drinks that had stained their white suits. Others worried the saucers would return and strike them. You couldn't recognize the place. The awning sagged. *FÉ DE LA RADE* was all anyone could read on the banner in flight along the sea wall. The photographers claimed to have proof. But when they developed their proof sheets, their cameras captured not one saucer.

LE DRAPEAU

Le drapeau se mit à grandir. Il devenait un symbole
du triomphe des armes. Les troupes applaudissaient
ce prodige et les tambours battirent aux champs. Le
drapeau grandissait, grandissait. Il fallut que des hommes
se précipitassent afin de soutenir sa hampe qui devenait
colonne, ses couleurs qui se déployaient au-dessus des
cavaliers et des fantassins. Brusquement le vent changea.
La colonne de la hampe s'écroula, broya les fuyards qui
perdaient la tête et se ruaient les uns contre les autres. Et,
tandis que se taisaient les tambours et que des clameurs
se faisaient entendre, les chefs ennemis purent voir, à la
lorgnette, l'étoffe triomphale s'abattre et recouvrir d'une
grande vague les hommes dont l'épouvante provoquait la
houle.

THE FLAG

The flag began to grow. It symbolized the triumph of arms. Troops applauded this marvel and drums rolled. The flag grew bigger, grew bigger. Men had to rush forward to support the flagpole swelling into a column, its colors spreading over the cavalry and foot soldiers. Abruptly the wind changed. The flagpole toppled over, crushing the fleeing men, who lost their heads and stampeded into each other. When the drums went silent and the clamor could be heard, enemy leaders could see through their opera glasses the triumphant cloth collapse and submerge in a vast wave the men whose terror had provoked the swell.

LE MUR DU SON

Le mur du son était double. R y avait eu somme un mur du son qui était deux. H procédait de la manière suivante. Le premier mur invisible se laissait traverser par l'appareil et se durcissait ensuite jusqu'à devenir mur de bronze. L'appareil parvenait au second mur invisible, lequel, feignant de se laisser traverser, se distendait en une poche élastique. Cette poche s'allongeait, épousait les formes. Soudain le mur invisible se retendait et cette poche envoyait l'appareil comme une fronde sur le mur de bronze, où il s'écrasait, éclatait, se désintégrait.

SOUND BARRIER

The sound barrier was double. There was, in other words, one wall of sound that was two. It was like this. The first invisible wall allowed the device to pass through it, and then solidified behind it into a wall of bronze. The device reached the second invisible wall, which made as if to let it through, but instead became an elastic pocket, stretched to fit the form. Suddenly the invisible wall tightened up and the pocket slung the device back into the bronze wall, where it was smashed, burst, and disintegrated.

PIEDS D'OMPHALE

Si Hercule ne s'était habillé en femme, si Omphale ne s'était pas vêtue en homme, tout cela ne serait pas arrivé ou serait arrivé d'une manière différente et moins propre à tromper l'Amour qui porte un bandeau sur les yeux. Pour un aveugle, même dieu, même d'une grande adresse a l'arc, il est impossible de distinguer le sexe faible du sexe fort, et facile de se perdre au milieu de l'enchevêtrement du fil de la massue changée en quenouille. Cette massue et cette quenouille furent l'origine des erreurs qui firent dupe un immortel se vantant de ne jamais l'être.

Éros devait s'expliquer dans la suite. Il aurait pris la quenouille pour une massue entourée de laine par le couple redoutable. Hercule, disait-il, n'avait qu'à filer. A filer sur les pieds d'Omphale.

FEET OF OMPHALE

If Hercules hadn't dressed as a woman, if Omphale hadn't dressed as a man, none of it would have happened, or it would have happened differently, and in a manner less able to fool blindfolded Love. For someone blind, even winged, even though a god, even though a great archer, it's impossible to distinguish the weak sex from the strong sex, and easy to be tangled in the snarled threads of a club used as a spindle. This club and this spindle fooled an immortal who boasted he could never be fooled.

Eros had to explain himself afterward. He mistook the spindle for a club wrapped in wool by the fearsome couple. Hercules, he said, had only to spin. To run off on the feet of Omphale.

L'ART

On fait ce qu'il ne faut pas faire et les faux pas et la maladresse en affaires et la malade enceinte qui se dresse dans la malle en fer blanc en faisant semblant d'être feue après le vol des faisans et (en joue feu) l'arme et le vol des bijoux et l'ange en larmes et l'art qui se trompe de chasse à courre et court de meute en émeute et court trop court. Et comment la fausse feue se change en elle-même et comment se meut un feu Saint-Elme.

ART

We do what we shouldn't, the faux pas and business blunders, the sick pregnant woman who rises from inside a tin trunk, pretending to be dead after the flight of the pheasants, and (aim, fire) the weapon, the theft of the jewels, the angel in tears, and the art that hounds the wrong prey, runs in a wild pack and comes up short. How does the recently deceased become herself and how does St. Elmo's fire transport itself.

LE MOT

A travers quels chemins d'une carte insoumise au système fluvial des veines et des artères m'est-il venu ce mot tiré de moi par la fourche du coudrier? Par quels chemins m'est-il venu avec sa gueule de haine, les armes et les documents aptes à me perdre, à convaincre les juges de mon innocence contre laquelle il n'existe aucun recours.

Si je l'efface il imitera les termites. Il ruinera les moelles de l'édifice. Sa rage vient de ce qu'il exécute les ordres d'un organisme qui vous emploie et vous abandonne après. S'il me manque on ne le manquera pas. Il sera victime de quelque vocable plus dangereux encore, sollicité par mon imprudence.

THE WORD

From which paths on an intractable map of a riverine system of veins and arteries was this word pulled from me by a forked hazel wand? By which route did it come to me, its hateful face, weapons and documents apt to undo me, to convince the judges of my innocence against which there is no appeal?

If I erase it, it will swarm like termites and destroy the core of the building. Its cravings follow the commands of an organism that uses you then dumps you. If I miss it, we won't miss it. It will succumb to some even more dangerous term, called forth by my carelessness.

LE RIRE

Le rire éclatait et blessait les spectateurs d'un cercle de curiosité dans la rue. Il énervait la police à cause de cette sensation désagréable d'être vue par le meurtrier invisible et attentif au moindre entrefilet de son journal. Et le rire les aspergeait tous de gerbes méchantes, à telles enseignes que certaines personnes du premier rang criaient: « Prenez garde » et reculaient, piétinant les autres.

La curiosité satisfaite, le rire resta seul et cessa de rire. Il n'y avait pas de quoi rire. Les pavés étaient rouges d'une graisse gluante et dégoûtante. Et le chef de la police confiait à ses collègues: « Je voudrais bien savoir pourquoi ce rire a ri ».

THE LAUGH

The laugh exploded and injured curious spectators circling it in the street. It annoyed the police, who had the disagreeable sensation that the invisible murderer was watching them while scanning his newspaper for the tiniest news of his crime. The laugh drenched them all with so much noxious spittle that certain people in the front cried, "*Watch out!*" and surged backward, trampling the others.

Curiosity satisfied, the laugh stood alone and stopped laughing. There was nothing to laugh about. The paving stones were stained red with sticky, repulsive grease. The police chief confided to his colleagues, "*I really want to know why that laugh laughed.*"

LE PETIT HOMME

Peut-être — enfin je ne sais pas — sans doute — malgré l'atrocité du crime — Peut-être (dis-je) — il est possible — il eût été préférable — de très grandes empreintes ayant dérouté les recherches, que ces recherches, que le champ de plus en plus étroit de ces recherches, que cette battue en cercle autour du seul point où se pussent tenir debout les pieds du criminel, après plusieurs mois d'incertitude et d'un tube de pâte funeste aplati jusqu'à ne laisser paraître que le coupable, n'aboutissent pas à la découverte de ce petit bonhomme dont l'apparence relève davantage de la comédie que du drame, à cette solitude motivant plutôt le rire que l'épouvante.

THE LITTLE MAN

Maybe — actually I don't know — certainly — despite the horror of the crime — Maybe (as I say) — it's possible — it would have been preferable — some very big footprints having thrown off the investigation, that these investigations, that the focus of these investigations having become narrower, that this hunt circling around a single spot where the criminal's feet could have stood, after several months of uncertainty and a dreadful tube of paste flattened to squeeze out only the guilty, would not lead to the discovery of this little man whose appearance gives rise to comedy rather than drama, to a solitude more risible than horrifying.

SCÈNE DE MÉNAGE

La comtesse s'écria: «Vous osez!» Le comte: «J'ose». La comtesse le frappa sur la tête. Et il y eut un cataclysme que la Bible enregistre sous la formule H.2.O.C.A.B.L. Des îles surgirent. Des montagnes s'effondrèrent. Des vagues couvrirent les continents qui changèrent de forme. Les pôles inversèrent leurs axes. Et ce n'était pas la faute de la comtesse. Elle ignorait qu'elle était un *nombre* et que ce nombre faussait les calculs de l'ange qui travaillait, penché sur son pupitre. Qu'y pouvait la comtesse? La malheureuse! Et le comte, cette victime. Et le monde, le grand monde, qui ne s'attendait pas à ce que la comtesse changeât de cycle, car elle était riche, élégante et joueuse de cartes. Son mari jouait aux courses et au golf. Qui pouvait se douter des suites d'une scène de ménage. Qui? Sinon la Grande Ourse qui se croyait petite et le triangle qui se croyait ovale et la ligne droite qui se croyait courbe, et le zéro qui proclamait: *Je suis le chiffre trois.*

DOMESTIC SCENE

The countess cried, "You dare!" The count, "I dare." The countess struck him on the head. There resulted a cataclysm registered in the Bible under the formula H.2.O.C.A.B.L. New islands surged from the sea. Mountains crumbled. Waves flooded the continents and reshaped them. The poles inverted their axis. And it wasn't the countess's fault. She had forgotten she was a *number* and was skewing the angel's calculations as he bent over at his desk. What could the countess do? Poor thing! And the count, that victim. And the world, the great world that had not expected the countess to change her cycle, since she was rich, elegant and played cards. Her husband played the horses and golf. Who could imagine the fallout from this domestic scene. Who? Other than the Great Bear that thought itself small, and the triangle that thought it was an oval, and the straight line that thought it was curved, and the zero, which proclaimed: *I am the number three.*

LES CHIMISTES DES ÎLES SANGUINAIRES

Le silence se retourna comme un gant par la faute de quatre chimistes sur la plage d'une des îles Sanguinaires. Ces hommes casqués d'une bulle de gaz dont les irisations marécageuses laissaient apercevoir la crainte, entendirent une muraille de vacarme s'élever entre eux et tout, avec une vitesse comparable à la lenteur. Cette muraille poussait le cri des anges de l'Apocalypse. Les bulles de gaz n'éclataient pas. Leurs membranes mouvantes permettaient aux chimistes de suivre les phases d'un écroulement qui se produisait à l'inverse d'une chose qui croule, qui s'écroulait vers le haut. Le soleil, les vagues, le sable, conservaient une sournoise indifférence. Seules des espèces de mouettes tombaient du ciel, mortes. Le vacarme à peine atténué par le gaz devenait intolérable. Alors un des chimistes arracha le fil qui reliait deux boîtes de cuivre et l'écroulement se produisit de haut en bas. Le silence redevint silence. Les quatre hommes quittèrent leurs casques et il ne resta du sinistre que les cadavres des mouettes sur la mer.

CHEMISTS ON THE ÎLES SANGUINAIRES

Silence turned itself inside out like a glove because of four chemists standing on the beach of one of the îles Sanguinaires. These men, each helmeted with a gas bubble whose swampy iridescence allowed them to see fear, heard a deafening noise rise up like a wall around them with a speed that seemed slow. It was the cry of the Angels of the Apocalypse. The gas bubbles did not burst. Through their flexible membranes, the chemists followed the stages of a collapse-in-reverse, going from the bottom to the top. The sun, the waves, the sand, preserved a sneaky indifference. Seagulls of some kind fell dead from the sky. Roaring, only slightly dampened by the gas, became unbearable. So one chemist pulled out the wire between two copper-clad boxes; the crumbling reversed itself, going from top to bottom. Silence again became a real silence. The four men removed their helmets; no sign of the disaster except for the corpses of gulls on the sea.

LE TABLEAU NOIR

Le son n'était pas arrivé. L'image cria: «*Nous sommes partis en même temps.*» Le son traînait toujours en route. «*Je ne l'attendrai pas*», disait-elle. L'image était en couleurs et insupportable. Le son tardait exprès. Mais l'image refusa d'attendre. Il en résulta que le son et l'image ne purent se rejoindre. Des chiffres à la craie en témoignent avec exactitude. Le son avait traité l'image d'hypoténuse et autres douceurs, car l'image se vantait de sa vitesse et le son prétendait que, s'il le voulait, il arriverait avant elle. C'est la scène que représente un célèbre tableau d'Einstein appelé par le Musée d'Art Moderne de New-York: *le Tableau Noir*.

THE BLACKBOARD

The sound hadn't arrived. The image cried, "*We left at the same time.*" The sound dragged en route. "*I won't wait for it,*" the image said. The image was in color and being insufferable. The sound delayed on purpose. But the image refused to wait. As a result the sound and the image never met up. Chalk figures kept an exact tally. The sound called the image a hypotenuse and other endearments; the image boasted about its speed; the sound claimed that if it wanted to it could get there first. That's the scene represented in Einstein's famous painting titled "The Blackboard" in New York's Museum of Modern Art.

MYTHOLOGIE

Les cheveux en serpents ou « serpents cheveux » de la gorgone Méduse, eurent une étonnante facilité calculatrice, bouclant des chiffres, les bouclant et les débouclant et calculant des calculs qui se posaient et se résolvaient dans sa tête et devenaient ensuite une onde propre à statufier les humains. Ces chiffres étaient notés par la gorgone Sthéno, sœur de Méduse, extraordinairement adroite à les prendre au vol et à les transcrire par signes sur ses tablettes, où elle notait en outre le nombre des victimes de la pétrification. C'est mortes de fatigue à la suite de calculs, qu'elles s'endormirent, que Persée coupa cette tête pleine de chiffres d'où naquit Pégase et dont les chiffres devinrent poèmes. Cette tête pétrifiante se trouve actuellement sur le bouclier d'Athéna, créatrice du musée d'Athènes et de tous les musées de sculpture antique.

MYTHOLOGY

The Gorgon Medusa's snaky hair or "snake hairs" were astounding calculators, crunching numbers, curling and uncurling them, calculating calculations posed and resolved in her head, and pulsing a wave that turned humans into statues. The numbers were recorded by the Gorgon Stheno, sister of Medusa, extraordinarily skilled at snatching them from the air and transcribing them onto her tablets, noting the number of petrified victims. When they were asleep, exhausted to death by all that calculating, Perseus cut off the head full of numbers, which gave birth to Pegasus and turned the numbers to poems. You can actually find her petrifying head on the shield of Athena, creator of the Athens Museum and all the museums of ancient sculpture.

SAUVE QUI PEUT

«*Sauve qui peut!*» N'entendirent-ils pas, ou ne voulurent-ils pas entendre? Ils continuaient la lutte gréco-romaine sur la plage. D'autres, assis, réparaient les filets maintenus par les orteils. Les femmes cuisaient la soupe. Elles activaient avec leur bouche la braise des fours de briques. La voix avait pourtant crié de toutes ses forces. Ils ne l'entendirent pas ou ne voulurent pas l'entendre. En une seconde les lutteurs, les pêcheurs, les femmes, se pétrifièrent, devinrent des objets d'art gracieux et terribles. Alors Minerve s'avança sur la digue, son bouclier à la main. Jason marchait assez loin derrière elle. Et de la même voix qui avait crié, il criait: «*Ce n'est pas votre faute. Je les avais prévenus.*»

SAVE YOURSELVES

"*Save yourselves!*" Had they not heard, or had they not wanted to hear? They continued their Greco-Roman wrestling match on the beach. Others sat repairing nets they held in place with their big toes. The women cooked soup. They blew on the embers in their brick ovens. The voice had cried out with all its strength, but they did not hear it, or did not want to hear it. Instantly, the wrestlers, the fishermen, and the women turned to stone, became graceful and terrible objects of art. Whereupon Minerva approached on the seawall, her shield in her hand. Jason followed from a distance. In the same voice that had cried out, he called to her, "*It's not your fault. I warned them.*"

LES GÉMEAUX

Bien imbriqués de bras et de jambes, tête-bêche à l'exemple d'un jeu de cartes (sauf la ligne oblique convertie en volute intestinale) ils attendaient un signe ou cygne qui de son bec orange cassât l'œuf traversé d'un arbuste de corail. L'un à l'autre ingénieusement et gracieusement noués dans la ténèbre lumineuse, ils attendaient que des coups de bec brisassent la coquille convexe ou concave selon qu'ils y fussent blottis ou qu'un œil à la pointe du triangle noir devinât de l'extérieur la plénitude gélatineuse de l'habitacle. Parmi les herbes de la rive, l'œuf posé sur un point de son équilibre (sous l'œil d'une dame nue et cet autre œil au faîte d'un col sinueux attentif à l'éclosion) attendait que les gémeaux passassent du vertébré ovipare à l'humain et de l'humain au groupe d'astres fixes qui les représente.

GEMINI

Arms and legs entangled, head to tail like a playing card (the diagonal line converted to intestinal curl), they waited for a sign or a swan whose orange beak would break the egg crisscrossed with fans of coral. Ingeniously and gracefully knotted in the luminous darkness, they attended the crack of the shell—concave if you're snuggled inside, or convex if looking into the gelatinous fullness of their compartment from an eye at the point of a black triangle. Amid the grasses of the riverbank, the egg balanced on tip-end (under the eye of a naked lady and another eye atop a sinuous neck focused on the hatching), and waited for the twins to pass from avian vertebrate to human, and from human to the cluster of fixed stars that represents them.

DÉTESTABLES ACCROCHE-CŒURS

O détestables accroche-cœurs, accordéons, escaliers, éventails, chutes, écroulement de roses. Que la mort parle du nez cela ne fait pas l'ombre d'un doute. Le difficile est de l'entendre, parce qu'elle est sourde. On pourrait la reconnaître à sa figure de guitare. Mais, avant même qu'on n'y songe, la foule des masques nous bouscule et nous entraîne loin de nous.

DETESTABLE SPIT CURLS

O detestable spit curls, accordions, stairsteps, folding fan, free-fall, rose-petal drop. That death speaks nasally is beyond the shadow of a doubt. But is it hard to hear it, because death is deaf. You can recognize it by its guitar-shaped silhouette. But before we can even dream it, the masked crowd jostles us and sweeps us far from ourselves.

PORTRAIT DE FEMME

L'arête ou aile du nez menaçait la bouche par l'insecte noir des narines. L'œil était dessus et dessous. Le menton formait avec le col de linge une courbe qui se perdait dans le labyrinthe mystérieux de l'oreille. Le profil était de face à cause des ombres et d'une certaine lenteur de ses mouvements. Que dire d'une main droite si grande qu'elle cachait toute la figure par une volonté qui lui était propre et n'avait aucune attache avec celle de l'épaule par exemple ou de la cuisse ou d'un autre membre de cet échafaudage autour d'une âme construite par mille ouvriers médiévaux.

PORTRAIT OF A WOMAN

The ridge or wings of the nose threatened the mouth with the black insect of the nostrils. The eye was above and below. The chin formed a curve with the collar, losing itself in the mysterious labyrinth of the ear. The profile faced front because of shadows and a certain slowness of movement. What is there to say about a right hand so large it hid the whole face, with a will of its own not connected in any way to the shoulder, for instance, or the thigh or some other part of this scaffolding constructed by a thousand medieval laborers around a soul.

MINE DE RIEN

Qui bâtissait, qui démolissait dans ma carcasse? On sonnait d'une horrible petite trompette de rémouleur. Après quoi il y avait une attente et les mines explosaient en cassant toutes les vitres. Travail exécuté par des arabes, préoccupés d'en finir vite. Je ne savais jamais quand devaient se produire les explosions, sauf par le branle d'une foreuse qui m'assourdissait et préparait la pose des explosifs. Je dis des arabes parce que j'avais vu des arabes employés à ce genre de travaux. Mais ils étaient dehors et n'attaquaient que des roches. Ce dût être à l'exemple de ce spectacle que l'entreprise se mit à fonctionner en moi. Rien ne prouve qu'elle embauche des arabes. Peut-être s'en arrange-t-elle toute seule, experte à ruiner mon sommeil. Toujours est-il que je redoute le signal de l'horrible petite trompette.

BLANK LOOK

Who was building, who demolishing inside my carcass? Someone sounded the horrible little trumpet announcing the knife grinder. A lull, and then mines exploded, blowing out the windows. The work of Arabs, hurrying fast to finish. I could never predict these explosions, except when that drilling sound deafened me while the explosives were set. I say Arabs because I saw some Arabs doing that kind of work. But they were outdoors and attacked nothing but some rocks. It must have been that spectacle that set this process in motion inside me. I have no proof that the enterprise employs Arabs. Maybe it happens all by itself, expertly wrecking my sleep. Nevertheless I always dread the signal of that horrible little trumpet.

LIVRE DE BORD

Le public arriva en retard au théâtre qui jouait en ma personne et il y faisait une obscurité pénible pour tout le monde. Surtout pour les artistes qui ne voyaient pas le public et le public avait grand'peine à les voir, trop occupé à lire le programme dans les ténèbres et à manger des bonbons entourés d'une sorte de papier-vacarme qu'on vendait à seule fin de troubler le silence. Le spectacle s'annonçait mal. Il se déroula sur ce mode. Il y avait en outre un orchestre qui habitait une fosse et ne pouvait pas jouer car le public envoyait du pain de seigle et des épluchures dans cette fosse d'orchestre, la croyant à l'usage de bêtes dangereuses et féroces. Le rideau rouge montait, descendait comme la guillotine. Il décapitait les artistes saluant et offrant imprudemment leurs cous. La presse déclara que ce spectacle était inepte et inapte à prendre sa place dans l'Histoire. Les machinistes s'affairaient et roulaient les voiles. Ils étaient effrayés par la tempête, par les oiseaux criards qui s'abattaient sur les planches. Flagellés par les vagues ils devenaient aveugles et incapables d'obéir aux ordres du capitaine.

LOGBOOK

The public arrived late to the theater inside my body, where everyone sat in uncomfortable darkness. Especially the artists who couldn't see the public, and the public who could hardly see them, too busy reading their programs in the gloom and eating their bonbons wrapped in a kind of noise-making-paper that is sold specifically to disturb the silence. The show began badly. It continued in this fashion. Making matters worse, an orchestra lived in the orchestra pit and could not play because the audience kept throwing in pieces of rye bread and peelings, believing there were fierce dangerous beasts in there. The red curtain rose, then fell like a guillotine. It decapitated the artists reckless enough to offer their necks and take a bow. The press declared that this spectacle was inept and unapt to take its place in History. The sceneshifters got busy furling some screens. They were afraid of the storm, of the birds that threw themselves screeching against the boards. Whipped by the waves they went blind, unable to follow the captain's orders.

PROSE EN VERS

Fer rouge d'un croc double et de pinces s'il n'av
Ait, d'une balle rougie à blanc et d'un tir
A l'œil ouvert (l'autre fermé) pour un octave
D'un doigt à l'autre d'où le son ne peut sortir

Osé, risqué, perdu d'office (à moins que d'une
Chance construite en malchances d'un maladroit
Orchestre, l'ombre assise en face de la lune
Ne couronne un cheval à la place du roi)

Car à ce jeu d'échecs il tirait seul la courte
Paille, sur une épave outremer. S'il n'avait
Osé, risqué, pourquoi ce visage de morte
S'intitulerait-il « *Jeune fille au navet* » ?

Ç'aurait été la débâcle de droite à gauche,
De bas en haut, de haut en bas et le milieu
Explosif détruisant ce que la mort ne fauche
Où s'échafaude en plein jour un spectre de lieu.

PROSE IN VERSE

A red-hot double-hook brand and pliers, if only he'd
Had them, a white-hot bullet, shot one eye open
(The other shut), an octave reaching from one
Finger to the next from which the sound can't escape,

Dared, risked, officially lost (at least a chance
Among all the mischances of a ham-fisted orchestra
That the shadow sitting across from the moon
Doesn't crown a horse instead of the king)

Because in this game of chess, only he would pick
The short straw on a faraway shipwreck. Had he not
Dared, risked, why would the face in that death's
Head be titled "Young Girl with Turnip"?

It would have been a rout from right to left,
From bottom to top, top to bottom, the explosive
Core destroying what death does not mow down,
And in broad daylight, the ghost of a place erects itself.

LE JUGE

La haine que les poètes inspirent est si grande qu'on les
ligote sur des espèces de roues carrées et qu'on les lâche en
haut de pentes aboutissant à des fosses pleines d'animaux
féroces. Une joyeuse foule de kermesse assiste à ce supplice.
Rien ne l'amuse comme les soubresauts des roues carrées
jusqu'à la fosse où les animaux attendent. Il arrive que
des animaux féroces se couchent et lèchent les pieds des
victimes. C'est alors une colère de la foule qui insulte les
fauves et les traite de lâches. J'ai assisté à ce supplice chance
on ne m'accusait pas d'être poète, j'observai qu'un des
juges me regardait malveillance, du coin de l'œil.

THE JUDGE

The hatred that poets inspire is so great that we lash them to these square wheels and release them from the top of slopes to roll down into pits full of fierce animals. Joyous crowds at the church fair take part in this torture. Nothing amuses them more than the jolting square wheels rolling right into the pit where the animals await them. It happens that the fearsome animals lie down and lick the feet of the victims. That's when the enraged crowd hurls insults at the wild beasts and curses them as cowards. I've witnessed this torture. Luckily no one has accused me of being a poet. But I did notice one of the judges looking malevolently at me out of the corner of his eye.

CATAFALQUE

Le choc des Écus et des Couronnes. Les grands tournois à têtes d'aigle. L'œil crevé du Prince. La poussière des jupes de chevaux et de dames qui s'évanouissent d'amour.

Les siècles se fracassent les uns contre les autres en silence malgré leurs écharpes tricolores. Catherine de Médicis dormait assise debout sur un catafalque de pages. Et l'Histoire de France, malade, tournait les pages, un livre ouvert sur ses genoux.

CATAFALQUE

Clash of the Shields and the Crowns. Great tournament of the eagle heads. Gouged eye of the Prince. The dust on the skirts of horses, and of ladies who faint from love.

The ages smash against each other in silence despite their tricolored scarves. Catherine de Médici sleeps sitting upright atop her catafalque of pages. And the History of France, ill, turns these pages, a book open on her knees.

IL FAUT BIEN S'AMUSER UN PEU

Il faut bien s'amuser un peu, n'est-ce pas, entre deux syncopes. Il faut bien s'amuser un peu, loin du cercle de famille qui déjeune sur l'herbe rouge au bord de la route. Il ne manquerait plus que d'être attaché à sa chaise comme Ulysse et, comme Ulysse, de laisser aux Enfers davantage que sa culotte. Il faut bien s'amuser un peu et traverser les routes où pédale Mercure, multiplié par mille miroirs. Il faut bien s'amuser un peu et tirer la langue à la mort qui nous surveille et nous recommande de ne prendre ni froid ni chaud. Quelle gouvernante! Quelle colle! Il faut bien s'amuser un peu et suivre l'enfance et les peurs qui la font courir à toutes jambes jusque dans le fleuve. C'est le seul refuge possible pour éviter la gouvernante qui lui court après.

WE REALLY SHOULD ENJOY OURSELVES A LITTLE

We really should enjoy ourselves a little, shouldn't we, between the two blackouts. We should enjoy ourselves a little, away from the family picnicking in the red grasses by the side of the road. The last thing we need is to be tied to our chair like Ulysses and, like Ulysses, leave to the Devil more than his pants. We should be enjoying ourselves a little, crossing the routes that Mercury pedals, multiplied in a thousand mirrors. We should be amusing ourselves a little and stick out our tongues at death, who watches us and warns us not to get too hot or too cold. What a governess! How clingy! It's necessary to amuse ourselves a little, to follow childhood and the fears that send it running full speed to the river. It's the ultimate refuge from that governess hot on its heels.

LANTERNE SOURDE

Ma solitude entourée de refus. Le vide où tombe de haut une cascade écœurante. Le juge en robe rouge que je porte en moi et qui me condamne à mort. Cette écume de détresse au bord des dents. Cette boule dans la gorge. Cette poitrine où s'amassent les orages qui n'éclatent pas. Cette route blanche qui me paralyse. Les hommes libres qui circulent dessus. Ce fleuve d'hommes libres autour de mon bagne. Tous ces magots qui remuent la tête de droite à gauche, de gauche à droite, et disent « non ». Et mon rire dans le noir. Ce rire qui aveugle ma lanterne sourde.

DARK LANTERN

My solitude encircled by refusal. Emptiness into which a sickening waterfall pours from a great height. The red-robed judge I carry within me who condemns me to death. This scum of distress at the edge of my teeth. Lump in my throat. Breast where storms gather without bursting. This white road that paralyses me. The free men who move on it. River of free men flowing around my prison. All those macaques writhing from left to right in my head, from right to left, and say "no." My laughter in the darkness. The laughter that blinds my dark lantern.

VARIANTE

Le corbeau perchait sur un buste de cet Héraclite, lequel, paraît-il, était maigre et portait barbiche. Le corbeau disait: « Quatre. Quatre ». Le buste répondait: « Trois ». Et avec ses vieux doigts jaunes le corbeau piétinait d'impatience la noble tête de marbre. « Trois. Trois » disait la noble tête de marbre. Et le corbeau répétait « Quatre ». Et ni le buste exsangue ni l'animal noir ne voulaient se laisser vaincre dans ce duel de verbe, duel qui risquait fort de s'éterniser. Il s'éternise. Toujours le corbeau répète « Quatre. Quatre ». Et toujours le buste répète « Trois ». Les mondes roulent. Les siècles se suivent. Les ruines se succèdent. Et dans la funeste bibliothèque le corbeau refuse de mourir et de s'avouer vaincu.

VARIANT

The crow perched on the bust of a certain Heraclitus, who appeared thin and wore a goatee. The crow said, "*Four. Four.*" The bust replies, "*Three.*" With its old yellow fingers the crow stamped with impatience on the noble marble head. "*Three. Three,*" said the noble marble head. The crow repeated, "*Four.*" And neither the bloodless bust nor the black beast would let itself be defeated in the verbal duel, a duel threatening to go on forever. It continues. Always the crow repeats, "*Four. Four.*" Always the bust repeats, "*Three.*" The worlds turn. One epoch follows another. Ruins follow, one after the other. In the dreadful library the crow refuses to die and admit defeat.

LETTRE D'ADIEU À MON AMI
FEDERICO

Chante. Par la bouche de ta blessure. Par la bouche entr'ouverte de ta blessure. Par la bouche grande ouverte de ta blessure. Par l'œillet mouillé cramoisi de ta blessure. Par la grenade luisante de ta blessure. Par le rire atroce du dentier d'un cheval de picador au soleil de ta blessure. Par le lait sombre des lèvres du nouveau-né de ta blessure. Par la lave du volcan de ta blessure. Par les muqueuses de l'oursin ouvert en deux de ta blessure. Par la caverne où se réveille en sursaut le gitan de ta blessure. Par l'étoile écarlate sur les ruines de ta blessure. Par l'encre rouge du dernier poème de ta blessure.

FAREWELL LETTER TO MY FRIEND FEDERICO

Sing. Through the mouth of your wound. Through the half-open mouth of your wound. Through the wide-open mouth of your wound. Through the crimson wet eyelet of your wound. With the glossy pomegranate of your wound. With the atrocious teeth in the laugh of the picador's horse in the sunshine of your wound. With the dark milk on the lips of the newborn of your wound. Out of the volcano lava of your wound. With the mucous membranes of an open sea urchin of your wound. Out of the cavern where the sleeping gypsy of your wound awakens with a start. With the scarlet star on the ruins of your wound. By the red ink of the last poem of your wound.

QUE DE CHOSES À DIRE...

Que de silex cassés en deux, que d'étincelles amères, que de têtes de mort éclatant autour de leurs orbites, que de chevaux riant de souffrance au soleil, que de coloquintes, de basilics, de mandragores dans la boue des sources profondes, que de pendus couverts d'oiseaux. Que d'épouvantails en croix. Que de jeunes filles bras dessus bras dessous dans l'effrayant parfum des usines de Nauplie, que de vagues qui crachent sur les rocs de Bretagne, que de sous-marins qui descendent rejoindre les trésors aveugles, que de clairs de lune cachés derrière un arbre, que d'ombres meurtrières qui les dénoncent. Que de choses à dire dans ce silence du vacarme des planètes et des hommes criant aux antipodes jusqu'à ce que notre lumière devienne la leur. Que de livres qui remplissent la Tour de Pise. Que de chutes qui attendent un signe. Que de grâces qui s'engloutissent dans la bouche d'ogre du zéro.

SO MANY THINGS TO SAY . . .

So many flint-stones broken in two, a shower of bitter sparks, so many death's heads bursting around their orbits, so many horses laughing with anguish in the sun, so many bitter apples, basils, mandrake roots in the mud of their deep wellsprings, so many hanged men covered in birds. So many crucified scarecrows. So many young girls arm in arm in the dreadful perfume of the factories of Nauplie, so many waves spitting upon the rocks of Brittany, so many submarines descending to rejoin the blind treasures, so much moonlight hiding behind a tree, so many murderous shadows informing on it. So many things to say in the noisy silence of the planets and the men crying poles apart just as our light becomes theirs. So many books filling the Tower of Pisa. So many downfalls waiting for a sign. So many graces gobbled by the ogre of zero.

AILLEURS

Qu'il était triste en écrivant ces lignes, recouvert préalablement de cette graisse du cygne sur un lac de fiente et de vase irisée. Qu'il était triste. Il naviguait sur l'encre de tous les stylographes vidés par l'altitude dans la poche des voyageurs. Il naviguait et souriait une espèce de grimace qui ne trompe personne à moins d'être aveugle et de lire le Journal des Voyages en caractères Braille. Les doigts des aveugles eux-mêmes étaient tristes. Cette lecture s'achevait en valses de Chopin et l'hôpital retentissait de la tristesse de leurs doigts. C'était un soir où les jours raccourcissent et traînent sur la mer en longue robe orange. C'était un soir où le lac s'irise de plus en plus à côté des égouts du bord de la mer. Et il sentait qu'il lui faudrait suivre le jour qui s'éloigne et chanter son chant de mort ailleurs.

ELSEWHERE

How sad he was while writing his lines, proactively coated with swan fat on a lake of birdshit and iridescent mud. How sad he was. He navigated on the ink of pens that had leaked into the pockets of travelers at high altitudes. He navigated and smiled a sort of rictus that fooled no one but the blind reading the Travel News in braille. The fingers of the blind themselves were sad. The reading ended with Chopin waltzes and the hospital echoed with the sadness of their fingers. It was a night when the days grew shorter and dragged upon the sea in a long orange gown. It was a night when the lake became increasingly iridescent next to the seaside sewers. He felt he should follow the vanishing day and sing his death song elsewhere.

*N*OTES

INTRODUCTION: Jean Cocteau kept an artist's journal of his work, which was published posthumously as *Le Passé defini* in 1983. Volumes I and II cover the years 1951 to 1953, and were translated as *Past Tense* by Richard Howard (New York: Harcourt, Brace Jovanovich, 1983 and 1985).

Henri Parisot (1908-1979) editor, translator best known for his anthology series for Fontaine, *L'Age d'or* (1945-1947), featuring the work of European and American authors with a surrealist focus. He reprised the series for Flammarion in 1964. Cocteau published *Opéra* in 1923 to great acclaim. *Appogiatures* begins with a dedication to him:

Dedicated to Henri Parisot.

My dear Parisot,
You've asked me to write these texts because you liked those in *Opéra*. They were to begin a new collection under your imprint. Circumstances require that my book appear on its own. But the texts are yours. I offer them to you as testament to our friendship, and of my respect for your services to the secret forces of poetry.
Jean Cocteau.

SOUND OF THE HORN: Puns on *cor* and *corps*, horn and body. And on *sac de son*: sack of sound and sack of "his." The expression, *on ne peut tirer de la farine d'un sac de son*, you can't get flour from a sack of sound, or you can't make a silk purse from a sow's ear.

CRIME OF PASSION: Read this poem aloud in the French too for its jazzy music.

SOIRÉE IN THE PRESERVE: A French-American pun: Eddy-proah or Oedipus, Americanized. The plot of Sophocles' *Oedipus Rex* features the image of the king's eyes gushing with blood. Jean Cocteau wrote the libretto for Igor Stravinsky's opera-oratorio *Oedipus Rex* in French; it was translated into Latin by Abbé Jean Daniélou, with a narration in the language of the audience. It premiered in Paris in 1927, and then in America the following year by the Boston Symphony and the Harvard Glee Club.

THE FRENCH LANGUAGE: A punning joke exploits French verb tenses. The marquise says, "... *je le susse,*" imperfect subjunctive of the verb "to know." Phonetically, it sounds like *je le suce*, present tense of *sucer*, to suck, or "I give a blowjob." Hence the hilarity of the young fool.

LIKE MASTER, LIKE VALET: Title alludes to *Tel père, tel fils*, "Like father like son." The seventheeth century French expression *Tirer le diable par la queue*, to pull the devil by the tail, means to make a deal with the devil to get out of trouble, especially financial trouble. In card reading, *valet de pique* or jack of spades is the conman of the deck, the knave, the trickster. He is the valet of the devil. The ace of hearts is the lover, ambitious for money.

THE PIANIST: *Jouer de la tompette*, playing the trumpet, is also slang for a playboy.

THE DENTIST: *fraise* means strawberry; *fraise dentaire* is a dental bur or drill.

THE ROMAN COACHMAN: The Domus Aurea was Nero's Golden Palace on the Palatine Hill in Rome.

POETRY SPORTS REPORT: A pun on *point*, meaning point (score) or period (punctuation).

THE TEACHER: A mix of English and French on the placard puns on *merci* or "thank you" in French, and "mercy" in English—a children's typo that is eloquent in its incorrectness. Also a pun on *se déguiser* to disguise oneself, and the Duc de Guise, sixteenth century nobleman and founder of the Catholic League, sometimes called Scarface (*Le Balafré*) after a battle wound. Descendent of Lucrezia Borgia and Pope Alexander VI, his royal ambitions were a threat to Henri III, who had him assassinated in 1588.

FÊTES GALANTES: A category of French seventeenth century rococo painting, typified by Watteau, depicting amorous couples in fancy dress cavorting in a parkland setting. The style reflected a shift from the grandeur of the church and royal court towards personal intimacy and sensuality. Composer Claude Debussy composed *Fêtes galantes*, songs for voice and piano, to the poems of Paul Verlaine in his 1869 collection of the same title.

THE SPA: *Ville d'eau* literally means a city of water, also a health spa.

THE REALIST GHOST: The phrase *dans une coulisse* can mean gliding on a runner or track, or backstage in a theater.

OSCAR: The "famous Oscar" also likely refers to Oscar Wilde.

FLYING SAUCERS: *Rade* means harbor; the café is the Harbor Café. *Fée* is fairy. Fé(e) de la Rade is a stranded or broken down fairy (*en rade*).

SOUND BARRIER: A *mur du son*, literally "wall of sound," is also "sound barrier."

FEET OF OMPHALE: Omphale, Queen of Lydia in Greek mythology, widow of King Tmolus, was the lover of Heracles. During his year of penitence for murdering

Iphitus, Heracles was sentenced to be her slave. He was forced to do women's work and wear women's clothing and hold her basket of wool while she spun it. Omphale wore his lion skin and carried his club. Later, Omphale freed him and married him. Apollinaire's poem "Hercule et Omphale" appeared in his erotic (and banned) novel *Eleven Thousand Penises, or the Loves of a Lord* (1907). *Filer* means to spin, also to leave or run off.

ART: Another poem that should be read aloud to hear the sonic wordplay.

DOMESTIC SCENE: A *scene de ménage*, domestic scene, also means a marital spat. Some wordplay: H.2.O.C.A.B.L., when pronounced in French, sounds like "A(r)che d' eau, c'est Abel": water arc or Noah's arc, it's Able (not Noah). The number 3 represents the Trinity: a sort of origin story.

CHEMISTS ON THE ÎLES SANGUINAIRES: An archipelago of four uninhabited islands off the coast of Corsica that becomes dark red at sunset, and when the leaves of the pink-flowered seaheath (*Frankenia laevis*) turn crimson in autumn.

THE BLACKBOARD: A *tableau* is a painting; *tableau noir*, literally a black painting, is a blackboard.

MYTHOLOGY: Some puns going on: *boucler des chiffres* means to add up or sum up; *bouclier* is a shield; *boucle* is a curl; *boucler* is to fasten, buckle, finish; *faire boucler* is to curl.

SAVE YOURSELVES: Greco-Roman wrestling, the style of wrestling based on a classical model, is practiced worldwide since the eighteenth century and at the Olympics since 1896.

GEMINI: *Les Gémeaux*, the astrological sign Gemini or the Twins; *jumeau* is twin. Also a pun on *signe* and *cygne*: sign and swan. The naked lady is Leda, raped by Zeus. Orpheus, an important figure for Cocteau, was transformed into a swan after his death and placed in the sky next to his harp, the constellation Lyra.

DETESTABLE SPIT CURLS: *Songer* means to dream, and to ponder or think something over.

PORTRAIT OF A WOMAN: Some punning wordplay: *dessus* and *dessous*, above and below. *Arête* is a ridge, an edge or a fishbone, *arrêter* is to stop; *ailes du nez* wings of the nose literally.

BLANK LOOK: There are puns on *mine*, meaning a bomb, a mine, or an appearance. *Mine de rien* means "a blank look" or "acting as if nothing happened" or "despite appearances."

LOGBOOK: *Voiles* are ship's sails, or theater screens. *Les planches*, the boards, is the floor of a stage or the deck of a ship.

PROSE IN VERSE: A pun on the title of the only lineated poem in the collection: *prose en vers* means lineated poetry, as opposed to prose poetry; *prose envers* is prose inside out, in reverse.

The poem draws from the children's song "*Il était un petit navire*": a little boat in which the starving sailors draw lots to decide which will be sacrificed. The youngest draws the short straw. Just as he's about to be eaten, a miracle causes thousands of fish to fill the boat, saving the boy.

A "turnip" is also a failure, something pale, uninteresting, dead. Referring to a film, it's a flop.

CATAFALQUE: Puns on *écu*, a shield and a coin, and on *couronne*, a crown and also an ancient coin; on *page*, a footman or the page of a book. The double-headed eagle represents church and state in the heraldry of the Holy Roman Empire. *L'Aigle à deux têtes* is the subject and title of a play by Cocteau in 1946 and a film in 1948.

DARK LANTERN: *Lanterne sourde*, literally a deaf lantern, is known in English as a dark lantern, a type of signal light that can be darkened with a sliding shutter. In French, it's also slang for a smuggler.

VARIANT: For Cocteau the number 4 symbolizes the earth; number 3 represents the sky.

FAREWELL LETTER TO MY FRIEND FEDERICO: This poem addresses Federico García Lorca, and refers to his assassination in 1936, and to the trauma of poetic creation. There is a pun on the word *grenade*, which means the fruit, pomegranate, and the explosive, a grenade.

SO MANY THINGS TO SAY: Nauplie is a town in the Greek Peloponnese.

*A*BOUT THE *A*UTHOR

Jean Cocteau (1889-1963), a French writer, artist, and film director, was one of the most influential creative figures in the Parisian avant-garde. He wrote poetry, novels, memoirs, plays, and operas and was a prolific illustrator, designer, painter, and sculptor. In the second half of his fifty-year career he produced and directed groundbreaking surrealist films, most notably *Blood of a Poet* (1930), *Beauty and the Beast* (1946), and *Orpheus* (1949). *New Yorker* film critic Pauline Kael called him "the progenitor of the new wave" of French filmmakers. By the end of his life he had published twenty-three books of poems, seven novels, seven screenplays, four memoirs, overseen twenty-one theater productions, including plays, operas, and ballets, twenty-six works with musicians, and eighteen films.

Born July 5, 1889, in Maisons-Laffitte, a suburb of Paris, Cocteau's Parisian household with his two older siblings was upended when his father, a lawyer and amateur artist, committed suicide when the boy was nine years old. His mother shared his growing passion for the arts; he would live with her off and on until her death in 1943. At the Lycée Condorcet in Paris, Cocteau developed a crush on the class bully, a boy he would eventually befriend, with the chiseled chin and burly physique that would become his ideal male figure in his art and films. At fifteen, Cocteau was expelled from school. He ran away to Marseilles, where he lived in the red light district under an assumed name until discovered by the police and brought home. His illustrated novel, *Le Livre blanc*, reflects his experiences there.

His career began in 1908 at age eighteen with his first published poem, "The Facades," performed in a public reading by the flamboyant tragedian Edouard de Max. The young poet took Paris by storm, attracting the support of writers like Marcel Proust. A year later he met the Ballets Russes impresario Sergey Diaghilev, whose 1913 production of *The Rites of Spring*, starring Vaslav Nijinsky, was life-altering for Cocteau. Diaghilev encouraged him to venture into other art forms, including the ballet, admonishing him, "*Étonne moi!*" ("Astonish me!"). Cocteau complied.

During World War I, in a custom-made uniform, he attached himself to a French unit on the Belgium front and drove an ambulance illegally until he was arrested and sent back to civilian life. Back in Paris he returned to his art. He wrote long poems; novels such as the surreal *Le Potomak*, and *Thomas l'imposteur* about his wartime experience; the plays *Orphée* and *Les Enfants terribles*; and ballets like *Parade*, a ground-breaking production in collaboration with Erik Satie and Pablo Picasso. His first film, *The Blood of a Poet*, came out in 1930. Despite the variety of his artforms, Cocteau considered himself a poet first, saying, "I am, without a doubt, the least known of poets and the most famous."

Cocteau's affair with the precocious fifteen-year-old novelist Raymond Radiguet, whom he discovered and nurtured as a writer, began in 1918 and ended with the boy's death five years later of typhoid. The loss triggered a fifteen-year addiction to opium and precipitated artistic dry spells alleviated by cures at health clinics where he could paint, draw, and write unimpeded.

At the end of World War II in 1945, Cocteau met Jean Marais, a young film star who would inspire some of his most successful movies. Besides *La Belle et la bête*, he directed or wrote the screenplays for *The Eagle with Two Heads*, *Les Enfants terribles*, *The Storm Within*, and the award-winning *Orpheus*.

His circle of friends and associates with whom he often collaborated grew ever wider, making up a who's who of European artistic life—Pablo Picasso, Guillaume Apollinaire, Erik Satie, Igor Stravinsky, Sergei Diaghilev, Louise de Vilmorin, Max Jacob, Blaise Cendars, André Gide, Jean Genet, Coco Chanel, and Colette. When Colette died in 1954, he took her seat at the Royal Academy of Belgium. In 1955, he was made a member of the Académie française. He was elected president of the Cannes Film festival for two years running.

Jean Cocteau died of a heart attack on October 11, 1963, at his chateau in Milly-la-Fôret after hearing the news of the death of his friend Edith Piaf.

ABOUT THE TRANSLATOR

Mary-Sherman Willis's books of poems include *Caveboy* (Artist's Proof Editions), and *Graffiti Calculus* (CW Books). Her poems, essays, and reviews have appeared in *American Scholar*, *Gargoyle*, *The Hudson Review*, *The Iowa Review*, *New Republic*, *Poet Lore*, *Shenandoah*, and *Southern Poetry Review*, among other publications; in Ted Kooser's column "American Life in Poetry"; and in various anthologies. She is a graduate of the Warren Wilson MFA Program for Writers and has taught creative writing at George Washington University. You may see more of her work at maryshermanwillis.com.

OTHER INTERNATIONAL EDITIONS BOOKS

Kajal Ahmad (Alana Marie Levinson-LaBrosse, Mewan Nahro
    Said Sofi, and Darya Abdul-Karim Ali Najin, trans., with
    Barbara Goldberg), *Handful of Salt*
Keyne Cheshire (trans.), *Murder at Jagged Rock: A Tragedy by
    Sophocles*
Yoko Danno & James C. Hopkins, *The Blue Door*
Moshe Dor, Barbara Goldberg, Giora Leshem, eds.,
    The Stones Remember: Native Israeli Poets
Moshe Dor (Barbara Goldberg, trans.), *Scorched by the Sun*
Lee Sang (Myong-Hee Kim, trans.), *Crow's Eye View:
    The Infamy of Lee Sang, Korean Poet*
Vladimir Levchev (Henry Taylor, trans.), *Black Book of
    the Endangered Species*

THE TENTH GATE PRIZE

Jennifer Barber, *Works on Paper*, 2015
Roger Sedarat, *Haji as Puppet*, 2016
Lisa Sewell, *Impossible Object*, 2014

Nathalie F. Anderson, *Following Fred Astaire*, 1998
Michael Atkinson, *One Hundred Children Waiting for a Train*, 2001
Molly Bashaw, *The Whole Field Still Moving Inside It*, 2013
Carrie Bennett, *biography of water*, 2004
Peter Blair, *Last Heat*, 1999
John Bradley, *Love-in-Idleness: The Poetry of Roberto Zingarello*, 1995,
    2nd edition 2014
Christopher Bursk, *The Way Water Rubs Stone*, 1988
Richard Carr, *Ace*, 2008
Jamison Crabtree, *Rel[AM]ent*, 2014
Jessica Cuello, *Hunt*, 2016
B. K. Fischer, *St. Rage's Vault*, 2012
Linda Lee Harper, *Toward Desire*, 1995
Ann Rae Jonas, *A Diamond Is Hard But Not Tough*, 1997
Frannie Lindsay, *Mayweed*, 2009
Richard Lyons, *Fleur Carnivore*, 2005
Elaine Magarrell, *Blameless Lives*, 1991
Fred Marchant, *Tipping Point*, 1993, 2nd edition 2013
Ron Mohring, *Survivable World*, 2003
Barbara Moore, *Farewell to the Body*, 1990
Brad Richard, *Motion Studies*, 2010
Jay Rogoff, *The Cutoff*, 1994
Prartho Sereno, *Call from Paris*, 2007, 2nd edition 2013
Enid Shomer, *Stalking the Florida Panther*, 1987
John Surowiecki, *The Hat City After Men Stopped Wearing Hats*, 2006
Miles Waggener, *Phoenix Suites*, 2002
Charlotte Warren, *Gandhi's Lap*, 2000
Mike White, *How to Make a Bird with Two Hands*, 2011
Nancy White, *Sun, Moon, Salt*, 1992, 2nd edition 2010
George Young, *Spinoza's Mouse*, 1996

THE HILARY THAM CAPITAL COLLECTION

Nathalie Anderson, *Stain*
Mel Belin, *Flesh That Was Chrysalis*
Carrie Bennett, *The Land Is a Painted Thing*
Doris Brody, *Judging the Distance*
Sarah Browning, *Whiskey in the Garden of Eden*
Grace Cavalieri, *Pinecrest Rest Haven*
Cheryl Clarke, *By My Precise Haircut*
Christopher Conlon, *Gilbert and Garbo in Love*
        & *Mary Falls: Requiem for Mrs. Surratt*
Donna Denizé, *Broken like Job*
W. Perry Epes, *Nothing Happened*
David Eye, *Seed*
Bernadette Geyer, *The Scabbard of Her Throat*
Barbara G. S. Hagerty, *Twinzilla*
James Hopkins, *Eight Pale Women*
Brandon Johnson, *Love's Skin*
Marilyn McCabe, *Perpetual Motion*
Judith McCombs, *The Habit of Fire*
James McEwen, *Snake Country*
Miles David Moore, *The Bears of Paris*
        & *Rollercoaster*
Kathi Morrison-Taylor, *By the Nest*
Tera Vale Ragan, *Reading the Ground*
Michael Shaffner, *The Good Opinion of Squirrels*
Maria Terrone, *The Bodies We Were Loaned*
Hilary Tham, *Bad Names for Women*
        & *Counting*
Barbara Louise Ungar, *Charlotte Brontë, You Ruined My Life*
        & *Immortal Medusa*
Jonathan Vaile, *Blue Cowboy*
Rosemary Winslow, *Green Bodies*
Michele Wolf, *Immersion*
Joe Zealberg, *Covalence*

OTHER WORD WORKS BOOKS

Annik Adey-Babinski, *Okay Cool No Smoking Love Pony*
Karren L. Alenier, *Wandering on the Outside*
Karren L. Alenier, ed., *Whose Woods These Are*
Karren L. Alenier & Miles David Moore, eds.,
    Winners: A Retrospective of the Washington Prize
Christopher Bursk, ed., *Cool Fire*
Barbara Goldberg, *Berta Broadfoot and Pepin the Short*
Frannie Lindsay, *If Mercy*
Elaine Magarrell, *The Madness of Chefs*
Marilyn McCabe, *Glass Factory*
Ann Pelletier, *Letter That Never*
Ayaz Pirani, *Happy You Are Here*
W.T. Pfefferle, *My Coolest Shirt*
Jacklyn Potter, Dwaine Rieves, Gary Stein, eds.,
    Cabin Fever: Poets at Joaquin Miller's Cabin
Robert Sargent, *Aspects of a Southern Story*
    & *A Woman from Memphis*
Fritz Ward, *Tsunami Diorama*
Amber West, *Hen & God*
Nancy White, ed., *Word for Word*

CPSIA information can be obtained
at www.ICGtesting.com
Printed in the USA
FFOW05n1620080117